Breaking the Chains
of
Psychological
Slavery

by

Na'im Akbar, Ph.D.

PRODUCTIONS

Mind Productions & Associates
324 N. Copeland Street
Tallahassee, FL 32304
(904) 222-1764

First Printing: August 1996
Second Printing: August 1997

Cover Design: Thomas Rasheed

Published by *Mind Productions & Associates, Inc.*
Tallahassee, Florida 32304

Library of Congress Catalog Card Number: 94-094434
ISBN: 0-935257-05-5

Dedication

*The Faith of our Ancestors
and the Mercy of Allah*

Table of Contents

Introduction

The parent publication to this book was entitled *Chains and Images of Psychological Slavery* and was originally published in 1976. It was reissued with some minor revisions in 1984 and during the last dozen years, well over 120,000 of these books have been printed and sold. Despite the brevity and simplicity of the book, readers have repeatedly told us this is one of the most significant of the books we have written and distributed over the last 20 years. The significance of this book seems to have been the result of the fact that it directly identified a wide range of persisting problems which plague the African-American community. When these problems were traced to the African-American experience of slavery, they seemed to have made intuitive sense to so many of us who are the descendants of those slaves. Qualities which had been observed in our communities and in ourselves for generations seemed to fit with this formulation of being possessed by the "ghost of the plantation."

History cannot be reversed and this review of the circumstances of the slavery of the African in America was not intended to be the completion of this analysis. The 300-year captivity of Africans in America is an indisputable fact which too many have sought to deny as relevant to anything more than an event of the past. Our formulation suggested that the blemish of these inhumane conditions persists as a kind of post-traumatic stress syndrome on the collective mind of Africans in America and though its original cause cannot be altered, the genesis can be understood. As is accepted in most insight approaches to mental healing (called psychotherapy), a confrontation of the original trauma and a restructuring of the mind's faulty adaptations to the assault can serve to correct these disturbed patterns of responding. The book was intended to offer insight into what had been collectively denied by the entire society as having any relevance to the psychological functioning of African-American people. With this insight, we believed that internal healing could begin. Over the last 20 years and with the thousands of people who have read just this book alone, some of the healing has begun.

Many people, however, have identified the demon in the past and have accepted the irreversibility of the mental slavery. We definitely wanted to give credibility to the reality of mental slavery. We did not want to suggest that it was irreversible neither because of its origin in the past nor because of its collective form. We wanted to help people know where the ghost came from but we wanted to destroy the ghost, not give safe refuge to it. Many people used the earlier form of this book to destroy the refuge of the ghost within their own minds and within their own communities, but many failed to see the ghost and many more failed to take up the challenge of ridding their minds of it. Therefore, this new volume seemed to be necessary on the 20th anniversary of the publication of *Chains and Images of Psychological Slavery*.

Breaking the Chains of Psychological Slavery repeats the same lessons from the earlier volume. The description of examples of persisting slavery-based behaviors remains just as it was in the earlier volume. For those readers who have read that book you will find that this is a review of the same points which were discussed. The addition which warrants the renaming of this revision is the inclusion of specific sections which address the process of eliminating the ghost of the plantation. We are still very much convinced that it is absolutely important to acknowledge the realities of slavery and to confront the impact of this historical trauma on our collective minds as African-Americans. We also believe that the objective of this recognition should not be a process of simply casting blame. It is clear that there were masters and there were slaves; there were captors and captives and the facts speak for themselves. It is not sufficient for the healing of the slave/captives to simply blame the master/captors. We believe that they and their descendants will require a collective healing as well, but this is an issue which the captives cannot accomplish for their former captors. We are convinced that recognizing the origin and the continued manifestation of this psychological bondage is the start of a self-healing process which we as a people must engage in both individually and collectively.

In this volume we outline, in very simple terms, some of the steps in which we must engage to break the chains of psychological slavery. Our goal is to take us beyond the simple recognition of the trauma and to begin the process of healing our minds so that we can be free of the slavery mentality. As we stand at the dawn of the 21st century we are confident that the last remaining obstacle to the complete mental liberation of African-American people is the failure to release ourselves from slavery. What is now necessary for the completion of our liberation cannot be accomplished by anyone but ourselves. The political, economic, military and even intellectual struggles have been fought and won to the point that we can expect solutions from those arenas. We must now understand that any future process in those arenas or in any other arena of human activity can only occur when we have been properly liberated in our minds. The objective of this volume is to advance us along that course.

In the introduction to the earlier edition of this book, which we have included in this volume, we pay tribute to the many people who helped make *Chains and Images of Psychological Slavery* possible. There is a new company of committed folks who we must thank for their contribution to *Breaking the Chains of Psychological Slavery*. *Rosalyn Nix* has been invaluable in transcribing speeches, word processing manuscripts, editing and doing all of the layout for this new volume. She has been an irreplaceable assistant to me in producing my books over the last five years. *Anwar Diop* offers many encouraging and challenging ideas which provoked the development of this book as he has with several others. As an assistant and a friend, he does more than the obvious in helping me to produce these volumes. *Professor Thomas Rasheed*, a truly gifted graphic designer, has worked patiently with me and has been able to design the remarkable cover which captures the intent of this volume. *Syidah Mu'min* and *Byron Thomas* have been the office staff who help us carry on the daily operations of *Mind Productions and Associates*. They have given so much with such minimal rewards and we thank them for their dedication. So many people who are nameless and faceless offer so much encouragement by their words, comments and letters, and I owe so much to so many for their contributions in this regard. As always, I am very grateful to my family, to our Ancestors and to the God of the universe for their presence and work through my life.

Na'im Akbar
June 26, 1996
Tallahassee, Florida

Introduction to 1983 Edition

Slavery is the modern genesis experience for Africans in the Western World. Contained in this genesis is much about the continued social, economic, political, and cultural reality of African-Americans. There is contained in this tragic drama the nucleus of a mind wrought with the agonies of oppression of the most inhuman form, and simultaneously, the image of man's greatest triumph over conditions of the flesh.

There is a certain hesitation about dwelling on events of the past. On the one hand, it creates an atmosphere of determinism which removes the volitional possibilities of people to alter their condition. It tends to excuse the perpetuation of past events which could be altered simply by initiative. It preoccupies people unnecessarily and purposelessly with old hurts, tending old wounds. It is an emotional tirade that ultimately provides no constructive solutions for the present. But those who deny the lessons of the past are doomed to repeat them. Those who fail to recognize that the past is a shaper of the present, and the hand of yesterday continues to write on the slate of today, leave themselves vulnerable by not realizing the impact of influences which do serve to shape their lives.

The chattel slavery of Africans in America for over 300 years serves as one of the saddest commentaries on man's inhumanity to man. The tales of this period of our history are so brutal and morbid that they will arouse vehement hostilities at the very thought of what occurred. The level of cruelty was incomparable to anything recorded in modern history, including the Nazi atrocities at Auschwitz, which were fleeting and direct, destroying bodies, but essentially leaving the collective mind in tact. The protracted and intensive atrocities of slavery have had a lingering effect and the pain of times past continues to call out from the genetic memories of those whose ancestors survived the test of slavery.

As cruel and painful as chattle slavery was, it could be exceeded only by a worse form of slavery. This worse form of slavery, along with the chattel slavery, is the subject of these two essays. The slavery that captures the mind and imprisons the motivation, perception, aspiration and identity in a web of anti-self images, generating a personal and collective self-destruction, is more cruel than the shackles on the wrists and ankles. The slavery that feeds on the mind, invading the soul of man, destroying his loyalties to himself and establishing allegiance to forces which destroy him, is an even worse form of capture. The influences that permit an illusion of freedom, liberation, and self-determination, while tenaciously holding one's mind in subjugation, is the folly of only the sadistic.

Imam Warith Deen Muhammad, the prominent African-American Muslim leader, brought an interesting new twist to religion for African-Americans during the early years of his teaching following the death of his father, the Honorable Elijah Muhammad. This new twist is an interpretative analysis of religion and social processes based upon the religious doctrine of the *Holy Qur'an*.

This is a new twist, not in the application of the *Qur'an*, because its use is nearly seventy years old in its influence in African-American communities. What is new is an intellectual and rational analysis of religion and its meaning, as opposed to the persisting emotionalism which has characterized much of the religious approaches of African-American religious leaders. This is not to say that we have not had relevant religious scholars. On the contrary, we have had some of the most outstanding religious scholars. The problem is that most of the scholars have only taught the surface and ritual of the religious images.

Imam Muhammad has brought the exegesis and social commentary out of the seminaries into the streets, and in doing so, has harnessed a new religious psychology in the African-American community. Based upon the questions which he has raised among the members of his religious community, questions have had to be raised and answered throughout the Islamic and Christian communities in general, but particularly in the African-American communities. The important factor is that the questions have not been confined to the religious sector, but have penetrated into the entire social, academic, political, and economic sphere. Several of these penetrating issues have been addressed in three previous collections of essays which I have done since 1976.

This booklet takes up two other such issues which have been stimulated by my study of Imam Muhammad's lectures and writings. His own manuscripts have well-demonstrated that he does not need an interpreter in order to transform his verbal statements into literal ones. He has aptly presented and extrapolated from his own ideas. I am neither a spokesman nor an interpreter of the work of Imam Muhammad.

I am a devoted student of *Truth* and I seek Truth wherever I can find it.

The efforts of this discussion and the ones which have been produced before are not intended to "parrot" Mr. Muhammad's ideas, but to apply my grasp of his ideas to my research and study of the human mind and soul. He has served as a catalyst for many of these ideas and he has certainly facilitated the crystallization of many of those ideas into meaningful concepts. But I must take full responsibility for any misrepresentations that may be made of his ideas. He certainly is not responsible in any way for my personal interpretations. The integration of his ideas into those of many other great thinkers who have influenced my perceptions is also my responsibility. These essays are written with a hope that he will be complemented by my efforts, but by no means are they prepared under his specific instruction.

The two ideas which are developed in these essays relate to the impact of slavery and the influence of Caucasian images for worship on the psychology of African-Americans. Over the last eight years, Imam Muhammad has frequently made references to the "ghost of the plantation," which haunts the psychological and social processes of African-Americans. Stimulated by these comments, the first essay identifies some sample characteristics which are neither exhaustive nor necessarily more critical than some other possible traits, but are illustrative of the kind of connection which exists between the historical realities of slavery and the contemporary, social, and psychological characteristics of African-American communities.

Throughout the essay, I caution against a simplistic, unidimensional analysis which would argue for a single psycho-historical analysis of African-American characteristics which come out of a multiplicity of causes. In highlighting the slavery influences, we are demonstrating a distinct determinant of African-American psychological functioning which makes us unique in some of the causative influences on our actions. We are also introducing a behavioral determinant which does not have great legitimacy in Western psychology, which is the notion that individual behavior can be influenced by collective factors which are also historically remote. A full appreciation of the uniqueness of people can emerge from an appreciation of such factors. The commonality in people's responses to certain environmental influences can also be demonstrated by the same data.

The second essay takes on a more theologically-loaded issue-- the influence of racial religious imagery on the psychology of people. This discussion takes on the old iconoclastic arguments that have plagued the Christian church for centuries. The approach that we take is not theological. Although we are clear in the Qur'anic and Biblical injunction against religious imagery, idols, etc., our argument is not an issue of religious dogma. Within the context of our discussion of the psychology of slavery, we are interested in identifying the enslaving potential of this religious imagery–particularly as it relates to the portrayal of the *Divine* in the facial and physical characteristics of a particular people.

We approach this problem from the vantage point of the racial group that is portrayed, as well as its impact on the ones not portrayed. Our position is that the portrayal of the Divine in the physical form of any people, is a potentially damaging influence on the psychological and spiritual development of human beings. We thoroughly recognize the rationale and the value of utilizing such figures as a corrective agent by some African-American religious groups. The fact that some people have chosen to retaliate in an affirmative fashion, by depicting the heavenly host in Black racial characteristics, in contrast to the Caucasian racial features which have characterized our view of religious figures throughout our Western history, represents a reasonable reaction. We commend those whose vision was broad enough to spot the destructive influence of these images on the psyches of non-white people.

On the other hand, as we transcend the dimensions of emotional reaction and begin to contemplate rational initiative, we must also be cognizant of the deleterious effect of these religious images on the psychology of Caucasians, and be careful that we do not duplicate the same arrogance of a "God-complex" within our lives that many Caucasians have created in theirs.

There are other characteristics of these religious images which also have a profound influence on the psychology of people which Imam Muhammad and others have discussed and I have discussed in earlier essays. The focus of the discussion is specific, however, and deals directly with the impact of the racial features of the imagery and the impact on the racial identities of people who experience the imagery.

These essays were based upon lectures which I presented in several contexts. The incentive for getting them transcribed into this literal form was a direct consequence of the persisting encouragement of *Imam Armiya Nu'man*, of *New Mind Productions*, who has remained an advocate for developing and publishing meaningful scholarly works from the Islamic African-American perspective. The specific efforts of his wife, *Zakiyyah Nu'man*, made the job more accomplishable by doing the typing for the manuscripts.

The whole thing would not have been possible had I not received a letter several months ago from a young man incarcerated in a Connecticut institution who offered his efforts to assist me in getting more materials out. I had explained to him the absence of financial and staff resources to get work done, and he indicated that he was willing to do whatever he could to assist me. I must admit some initial doubt, because many people offer but few deliver. I sent him some tapes, however, and was pleasantly surprised to receive completed transcriptions back from him in a matter of days. This was the contribution of *Adib Fahmee Al-Hamed*, to whom I owe a particular debt of appreciation. He stands as a symbol for the inability of walls to contain the determined spirits of true men. He also stands as another shining example of the power of Al-Islam to transform the lives of human beings and to bridge worlds both geographically and socially. We pray that Allah will continue to bless Adib F. Al-Hamed with the great success to which he is aspiring.

We are also hopeful that this publication will be a statement of gratitude to him, to the Nu'mans, to *Imam W. D. Muhammad*, and to my wife, Renee, for her continued support in this and all of my efforts in this struggle to be a human being in spite of...

Na'im Akbar
July 1, 1983
Tallahassee, Florida

Psychological Legacy of Slavery

Slavery was "legally" ended in excess of 100 years ago, but over 300 years experienced in its brutality and unnaturalness constituted a severe psychological and social shock in the minds of African-Americans. This shock was so destructive to natural life processes that the current generation of African-Americans, although we are five to six generations removed from the actual experience of slavery, still carry the scars of this experience in both our social and mental lives. Psychologists and sociologists have failed to attend to the persistence of problems in our mental and social lives which clearly have roots in slavery. Only the historian has given proper attention to the shattering realities of slavery, and he has dealt with it only as descriptive of past events.

Clark (1972) observes that most social scientists would object to a discussion of slavery as a "cause" of contemporary behavior because it happened "too long ago." Clark identifies the origin of this objection in nineteenth century conceptions of science articulated by the British philosophers Locke and Hume, and practiced by the scientific giant, Isaac Newton. Clark (1972) observes:

> *In the Newtonian scheme of things, "a body at rest remains at rest unless acted upon by some external force." The behavior (movement) of things was thought to be the consequence of some antecedent and external event. ...Newtonian conceptions of absolute time and space have so conditioned many of us that it is impossible for us to conceive of events that have occurred "long in the past" (e.g., slavery) as having as much effect in determining present behavior as those events of relatively "recent" occurrence.*[1]

Clark, in this monumental piece, argues that slavery, more than any other single event, shaped the mentality of the present African-American.

In order to fully grasp the magnitude of our current problems, we must reopen the books on the events of slavery. Our objective should not be to cry stale tears for the past, nor to rekindle old hatreds for past injustices. Instead, we should seek to enlighten our path of today by better understanding where and how the lights were turned out yesterday. We should also understand that slavery should be viewed as a starting point for understanding the African-American psyche, and not as an end point. Therefore, the study of the African-American psyche should include psycho-history, but it should not be exclusively concerned with events in the past.

The list of attitudes and reactions which we have inherited from slavery is probably quite extensive. We want to identify here only some of the more blatant and currently destructive attitudes which rather clearly show their origins in the slavery situation. Hopefully, a look at this tarnished legacy will serve as a stimulus for us to rid ourselves of these slavery ideas, both individually and collectively.

Work

One of the attitudes which has been passed to us from slavery is the rather distorted African-American attitude towards work.

Slavery was forced labor. Kenneth Stampp (1956) described the work of the slave occurring "from day clear to first dark." The day's toil would begin just before sunrise and would end at dusk. Stampp observed:

> *Except for certain essential chores, Sunday work was uncommon but not unheard of if the crops required it. On Saturdays, slaves were often permitted to quit the fields at noon. They were also given holidays, most commonly at Christmas and after crops were laid by.* [2]

Basically, however, work was a daily chore, beginning in early childhood and continuing until death or total disability.

The slave was forced to work under the threat of abuse, or even death, but the work was not for the purpose of providing for his life's needs. Instead, he worked to produce for the slave master. He would neither profit from his labor nor enjoy the benefits of labor. A good crop did not improve his life, his family, or his community. Instead, it improved the life and community of the slave master. Frederick Douglass (1855, 1970) describes the slave's work accordingly:

> *...from twelve o'clock (mid-day) till dark, the human cattle are in motion, wielding their clumsy hoes; turned on by no hope of reward, no sense of gratitude, no love of children; nothing, save the dread and terror of the slave driver's lash. So goes one day, and so comes and goes another.* [3]

Work, in a natural society, is looked upon with pride, both because it permits persons to express themselves and because it supplies their survival needs. As a natural form of expression, work is not too distinguishable from play. During slavery, work was used as a punishment. The need for workers was the most identifiable cause of the African-American's enslavement. Work came to be despised as any punishment is despised. Work became hated as does any activity which causes suffering and brings no reward for the doer. Work became equated with slavery. Even today, the African-American slang expression which refers to a job as a "slave" communicates this painful connection.

Over the course of generations, work came to be a most hated activity. Despite the fact that we are over one hundred years removed from the direct slavery experience, African-Americans still, to a great extent, hate work. Work is identified with punishment. Work is equated with inferiority. Stampp (1956) also observes:

> *Masters who had at their command as few as a half dozen field hands, were tempted to improve their social status by withdrawing from the fields and devoting most of their time to managerial functions...but most slaves never saw their masters toiling in the fields...*[4]

Consequently, slaves equated work with enslavement and freedom with the avoidance of work. Work was identified as the activity of the underdog and was difficult to be viewed with pride. Work is something approached unwillingly and out of necessity only. It is also a badge of disparagement. The ability to look successful without doing any identifiable work became the image of affluence of many street hustlers and pimps.

Many African-Americans have developed a variety of habits to avoid work, such as reliance upon gambling, and other get-rich-quick schemes. Some of the difficulty that we experience in generating independent businesses and institutions is because of our hatred of work. It is still difficult to view the long-term reward of sustained work as being adequate to erase the stigma of such toil. It is much easier to work (often considerably harder) for someone else and get a predictable periodic salary and a work schedule which lets one create an illusion of leisure. Every Friday evening until Sunday becomes "Emancipation Day" all over again.

There are some African-Americans who become over-dependent on welfare as a way of life because of this "work phobia." Often, considerable energy is put into schemes to avoid work because "real work" is so distasteful. This, too, can be related to the historical root of associating work with slavery.

Certainly, the historical origin of the hatred of work does not completely explain the African-American's orientation to work. Equally as relevant is the vast shortage of jobs and the many obstacles to receiving the same benefits from work as do other members of the society. Work is still geared toward community-building for others and not for African-Americans. In addition, the society itself has developed such a leisure orientation that work has come to be something to be despised by all members of the society.

It is important, however, for African-Americans to know that many of our attitudes toward work are a result of our slavery experiences. These negative experiences associated with work continue to function as unconscious influences on us that make us respond in ways which may be contrary to our conscious intention. Awareness of these influences and their source begins to free us from their effects. Our slang, our songs, our jokes, our attitudes, transmitted from one generation to the next, preserve these reactions as if they were acquired yesterday.

Property

The slave was permitted to own nothing or very little. Certainly, property and the finer material objects such as clothes, jewelry, etc., were reserved for the slave master. Douglass (1970) again observes:

> *The yearly allowance of clothing for the slaves on this plantation consisted of two tow-linen shirts--such linen as the coarsest crash towels are made of; one pair of trousers and a jacket of woolen, most slazily put together, for winter; one pair of yarn stockings, and one pair of shoes of the coarsest description. The slave's entire apparel could not have cost more than eight dollars per year. The allowance of food and clothing for the little children, was committed to their mothers, or to the older slave woman having care of them. Children who were unable to work in the field had neither shoes, stockings, jackets nor trousers given them. Their clothing consisted of two coarse tow-*

*linen shirts--already described--per year; and when these
failed them, as they often did, they went naked until the
next allowance day.*[5]

The slave master's fine house, beautiful landscaping, exquisite
clothes and objects were associated with his power and status. In the
same way that the slave looked upon his master with hatred and
resentment, he also resented and envied the master's possessions because
those possessions were associated with freedom and the power to direct
one's life, family, and community.

African-Americans have the slavery influence of mixed attitudes toward material objects and property. On one hand, those
objects are still associated with the master and his powers. Therefore,
there is a tendency to resent property and to take a secret (unconscious)
delight in attacking it. Certainly, some of our tendencies toward
vandalism and abuse of property have their origin in these experiences
with property. Property is still viewed as belonging to the "master" and
not to the "slave."

This finds additional expression when the African-American is
thrown into public housing and rented properties which are, in fact, still
owned by the descendants of slave masters. Vandalism is unconsciously
gratifying in that it acts out that long-present resentment of the master's
property. Given the persisting dependence on the "master," it is safer
to be neglectful of his property than overtly hostile towards him.

On the other hand, slavery produced an unnatural attraction to
material objects. The cast-off hat or dress passed down from the "Big
House" to the cabin, became a symbol of pride and status. By wearing
"Massah's" old hat or "Missis" old dress, one could play at being Massah
or Missis for a few fanciful moments. An illustration of this idea dating
back to slavery experiences also comes from Stampp (1956):

*The elegantly dressed slaves who promenaded the streets of
Southern towns and cities on Sundays, the men in fine
linens and bright waistcoats, the women in full petticoats
and silk gowns, were usually the domestic servants of
wealthy planters and townspeople. Butlers, coachmen,
maids and valets had to uphold the prestige of their white
families.*[6]

These material objects or dregs of property became equated in the African-American's thinking with the full power of freedom and self-determination which the master enjoyed. We can observe a similar pattern in our developing children who play at being mama and daddy by putting on objects of their clothing or other objects associated with them.

The legacy of such experience with property and materials, has made these objects powerfully influential in the lives of many African-Americans. Large sums of money are thrown away yearly on expensive flashy clothes and cars. Uncomfortable, impractical and showy items of furniture drain our budgets and fail to satisfy our longings because of this persistent wish to look like the slave master. Many of our judgments about people and their worth are disproportionately determined by what those people own or wear. We spend great energy and wealth acquiring these objects associated with power rather than real human, social, political and economic power. There is a frequent tendency to confuse tokens of power with genuine power, based upon the slavery experience.

It is not unusual for concerned efforts to obtain "real" political and economic power to be prematurely aborted by a strategic dispensation of tokens. Realistically assertive efforts to alter social structures to equitably accommodate America's former slaves have frequently been terminated by offering limited material goods to the major strategist and the movement dies.

The major thinkers and scholars (potentially our most powerful agents of change) in African-American communities are often neutralized by a pittance of material goods. This socially destructive phenomena has its roots deep in the slavery experience. Too often the leaders in our communities have equated a small trinket of material gain with "having arrived." That leadership is soon lost to the African-American community. It is a recurrence of the old image of wearing "Massah's" discarded hat and thinking that you are "Massah."

It is important that we caution the reader in considering these ideas that we remember these factors are only one aspect of what determines our behavior. The destructiveness and violence in the American society's present mentality fosters vandalism. The materialism which has overrun the Western mind certainly has had its effect on the African-American mind. We simply want to be aware of the predispositions which operate from within us and from our past which may influence us in ways we do not realize.

Leadership

Probably one of the most destructive influences which has grown out of slavery is the disrespect of African-American leadership. The allegory is seen throughout nature that the most certain way to destroy life is to cut off the head. From the turkey to the cow to the human being, the most immediate way to bring death to a body is to remove its head. This is especially true as a social principle. One of the things that was systematically done during slavery was the elimination of control of any emerging "head" or leader. Slave narratives and historical accounts are full of descriptions of atrocities brought against anyone who exemplified real leadership capability. The slave holders realized that their power and control over the slaves was dependent upon the absence of any indigenous leadership among the slaves.

Any slave who began to emerge as a natural head, that is, one oriented toward survival of the whole body, was identified early and was either eliminated, isolated, killed, or ridiculed. In his or her place was put a leader who had been carefully picked, trained, and tested to stand only for the master's welfare. In other words, unnatural heads were attached to the slave communities. They furthered the cause of the master and frustrated the cause of the slave.

The slaves were taught to view with suspicion natural leaders who emerged from among themselves. Such heads were identified as "uppity" or "arrogant," and were branded as the kind of trouble-makers who were destined to bring trouble to the entire slave community. This idea was reinforced by the public punishment of such indigenous leadership and any of his/her associates or sympathizers. The entire slave community was often required to carry an extra burden or be deprived of some small privilege, primarily because of such "uppity slaves."

Such practices rather firmly entrenched the opposition to natural leaders. They were often isolated by their own community, and were usually the victims of fellow slave "snitches" who reported to the master that someone was brewing trouble. The "snitches," having demonstrated their loyalty to the master, were usually promoted to the position of slave leader, and another grafted leader was born--i.e., with a slave body and master's head. The slave community was encouraged to view the greater power given to the master-trained leader as an indication of his superior worth as a leader. The master-trained leader was rewarded, praised and given privileges as an inducement for the slaves to follow this manufactured leadership.

The long generations of being conditioned to reject natural and strong leadership had not only stifled the development of such leaders, but African-Americans still respond by rejecting such leaders. Even outstanding leaders, such as Dr. Martin Luther King, Jr., were rejected and denied support by the African-American educated and professional classes of people in our communities. Dr. King was condemned in the early days of his civil rights campaigns as a "trouble-maker." Dr. King and many of the young ministers who spearheaded the *Civil Rights Movement* had to leave their denominational convention and form another one to escape the criticism of their traditional colleagues who saw their social activism as troublesome because it was troublesome to white people. Only after receiving recognition from increasing numbers of "liberal" Caucasians was he accepted as a leader. Powerful leaders who emerged from the ranks of the uneducated, such as Elijah Muhammad, never received wide acceptance among the educated classes of former slaves--despite the fact that he offered the most powerful economic and self-help program of that time. Contemporary "Negro" history accounts devote extensive coverage to Muhammad's trainees, such as Malcolm (X) Shabazz, while mentioning the natural head who was his teacher only in passing. This same pattern of rejecting indigenous leadership showed its head in the 1995 *Million Man March* when many traditional religious and political leaders rejected the leadership of Minister Louis Farrakhan because he wasn't approved by the white establishment. An important sign that this mentality is changing was the presence of over one million people at the "march" despite white disapproval of its indigenous leadership.

Such rejection of strong African-American leadership is as conditioned in us as is our fear and hatred of a burning cross. It is important to realize that such efforts to undermine effective African-American leadership is still an on-going part of the current society. The press, for example, fails to mention many of the outstanding accomplishments of indigenous African-American leadership. On the other hand, the least important statement from a "master-appointed leader" gains front-page coverage!

The other side of this issue of "grafted leaders" is that a realistically based suspicion of African-American leadership grew in our communities. Forced to reject natural leadership (in opposition to our natural survival instincts), and to accept oppressor-appointed leadership, compelled our communities to essentially suspect all leadership.

This suspicion is manifested in a rather pervasive disrespect for Black leaders, unless they come equipped with a supply of token or mystical power. The token power usually comes in the form of a limousine, some ostentatious clothing, and some rather impressive jewelry. The mystical power requires identifying one's leadership as having some kind of "divine legitimization." These leaders often gain considerable followings of an intensely emotional form.

The other "leaders" who gain strong support are projected by the "master's" media and press, and are often chosen from uninformed athletes, politically naive preachers or even entertainers. The leadership of such persons seldom extends beyond their faddish and transitory stardom. Meanwhile, all other forms of small scale and large scale leaders, indigenous and otherwise, are destroyed by suspicion and disrespect.

As a people, African-Americans must begin to recognize the disposition which has been conditioned in us to reject natural, effective leadership. If we understand that we have been programmed through our history to reject our natural heads, we may begin to become more conscious of recognizing true leaders. It can be easily demonstrated that the persistent distrust and limited support given to African-American leaders has its origin in the many inappropriate heads which have been affixed to our bodies historically.

The Clown

Another popular character which has its origin in slavery is the African-American clown.

One of the primary forms of remaining in favor with the slave master by the slave was to provide entertainment for the master and his household. It is easy to observe that man exults in his superiority over lower animals by teaching them to do tricks and to be entertained by those tricks. In much the same way, the slave owner prided himself in his superiority by being entertained by the slave. Writers have long pointed to the *jester*, the *clown*, or the *fool*, as the inferior one who was responsible for making his superior laugh. Using a person for your clown has always been one of the major ways to assert your dominance over a person. Mockery is one of the more sophisticated forms of humiliation.

Great favors of leniency and special rewards were given to the clowning slave. He enjoyed a special status above the other slaves because he kept his master entertained. Even the arts, music and dance, which had originally been used for cultural expression and community recreation, became devices which were used by the slave to protect himself from the master's anger. "Fiddler," in the TV drama, *Roots*, was a colorful example of this manipulative function of the clown. Clowning and buffoonery became one of the primary ways that the violent and abusive slave master could be controlled and manipulated. A laughing or satisfied master was less likely to be a violent master. Frederick Douglass observes in his autobiography:

> *In all the songs of the slaves, there was ever some expression in praise of the great house farm; something which would flatter the pride of the owner, and possibly draw a favorable glance from him.*
>
> > *"I am going away to the great house farm,*
> > *O yea! O yea! O yea!*
> > *My old master is a good old master,*
> > *O yea! O yea! O yea!"*
>
> *This they would sing, with other words of their own improvisation--jargon to others, but full of meaning to themselves.*[7]

The problem with this pattern, as with others we have discussed, is that this kind of response has long outlived its real usefulness. What began as a survival tactic under highly unnatural living conditions, has become a crippling part of the psychology of a people seeking to restore life and community to themselves.

An overwhelming number of popular media presentations involve African-American clowns. Comedy is valuable unless it is done to the exclusion of aspects of other facets of a people's life. The clear under-representation of serious aspects of African-American life in the popular media, suggests that even the former slaves prefer to laugh about themselves rather than improve themselves. The buffoon Martin Lawrence in the 1990's and the bug-eyed "J.J." on the program *Good Times* in the 70's are updates of the 1940's and 1950's Stephin Fetchit and Mantan Moreland. These clowns were updates on the slavery buffoon who mastered being funny to survive. This is not to degrade obvious talent of these master showmen, but to identify a force which has exalted the clown while degrading or ignoring the scientist or other artistic genius among African-Americans.

Entertainers and athletes are the popular heroes of the African-American community. Physical prowess or comic exploit are the only characteristics Black heroes are permitted to express. Intellectual acuity, prophetic vision, moral integrity, technological know-how, and managerial efficiency are characteristics seldom, if ever, portrayed. Consequently, the slave images of power persists. African-American children, as a consequence, strive to throw balls or croon on microphones, rather than seeking to explore the universe, discover cures for infectious diseases, or discover ways to feed the starving masses in Africa or India. Such a preoccupation with impotent images was a device to keep the slaves' aspirations in check. These ball players and singers are still rewarded with air time and salaries unimaginable while Black scientists and scholars are seldom shown and poorly paid. The consequence is that African-American young people see greater possibility on the court, field or stage than they even imagine for the corporate suite, laboratory, surgery theatre or computer lab. The current slave mentality still inhibits aspiration to be anything more than a clown. The clear exception is Dr. Bill Cosby, who used the clown's role only as a tool in the educational agenda from his mind and that of others, who were committed to the advancement of African-American life.

An even more common example of the modern slave clown is the person who feels the necessity to be a daily clown in his interactions with Caucasians. Many people have observed or experienced the African-American member of an interracial team serving as the entertainer over lunch or at the party. Somehow, the "token" African-American always manages to be the "funniest guy." It becomes an obsession on the part of the minority member to maintain favor with his colleagues by keeping them laughing. He often finds himself being urged: "Come on Sam, tell us a joke."

So another old pattern, with its roots in slavery, continues to bring rewards on the modern stage. Human beings are unable to be about the serious business of living and building societies if they feel compelled to always clown or entertain others. People do not take you seriously if you don't take yourself seriously. A sense of humor brings necessary balance to an organized life, but a life of humor blinds one to life.

Personal Inferiority

Let us consider another one of the most destructive characteristics from slavery. This characteristic is a sense of our inferiority as African-American people. This characteristic has been discussed by psychologists more than any other. It has been used as an explanation for nearly every aspect of African-American behavior. The self-hatred or low self-esteem of African-American people has certainly been overworked but is worthy of our consideration in this discussion.

The shrewd slave makers were fully aware that people who still respected themselves as human beings would resist to the death the dehumanizing process of slavery. Therefore, a systematic process of creating a sense of inferiority in the proud African was necessary in order to maintain them as slaves. This was done by humiliating and dehumanizing acts such as public beatings, parading them on slave blocks unclothed, and inspecting them as though they were cattle or horses. They were forbidden to communicate with other slaves which would have been a basis for maintaining self-respect. Many historians and slave narratives report how young children were separated from their mothers because the mother's love might cultivate some self-respect in the child.

Cleanliness and personal effectiveness are fairly essential in the maintenance of self-respect. The slaves were kept filthy and the very nature of physical restraints over long periods of time began to develop in the people a sense of helplessness. The loss of the ability to even clean one's body and to shield oneself from a blow began to teach the slaves that they should have no self-respect.

These things, combined with the insults, the loss of cultural traditions, rituals, family life, religion, and even names, served to cement the loss of self-respect. As the slave master exalted himself and enforced respect of himself, he was increasingly viewed as superior to the slaves. The superiority was based on the utter dehumanization of the Africans. The slave was forced to bow and bend to the slave owner and treat him as God. With the image of a Caucasian man even as God, and with all kinds of images of Africans as dirty and only half human, it was inevitable that a sense of inferiority would grow into the African-American personality.

Carter G. Woodson (1931) observed over a half century ago:

> *...to handicap a student for life by teaching him that his*
> *black face is a curse and that his struggle to change his*

> *condition is hopeless, is the worst kind of lynching. It kills one's aspirations and dooms him to vagabondage and crime.*[8]

This sense of inferiority still affects us in many ways. Our inability to respect African-American leadership, our persistent and futile efforts to look like and act like Caucasian people, is based upon this sense of inferiority. The persistent tendency to think of dark skin as unattractive, kinky hair as "bad" hair, and African features as less appealing than Caucasian features, come from this sense of inferiority. Our lack of respect for African-American expertise and the irresponsibility of many African-American experts comes from this sense of inferiority. The disastrously high Black-on-Black homicide rate is in many ways indicative of fundamental disrespect for Black life growing out of this same sense of inferiority. It is a simple fact that people who love themselves seek to preserve their lives—not to destroy them.

The fact that we remain as consumers and laborers, rather than manufacturers, planners, and managers, has a lot to do with the sense of inferiority. The continued portrayal in the media of African-Americans as clowns, servants, crooks, and incompetents maintain this sense of inferiority. The limited number of powerful and dignified images of African-Americans in the media and the community as a whole, reduces our sense of self-respect. This is a continuation of the slavery patterns. Only those persons who looked like, acted like, and thought in the frame of reference of the master, were completely acceptable. Those earning such acceptance were projected as far superior to those who looked like, acted like, and thought in the frame of reference of African self-affirmation.

We can reverse the destructive effects of slavery by looking to strengths in our past and beginning to make plans for our future. If we begin to direct our children's attention to strong images like themselves, they will grow in self-respect. We must honor and exalt our own heroes and those heroes must be people who have done the most to dignify us as a people. We must seek to overcome the "plantation ghost" by identifying the forces which lead to enslavement and self-abasement. We must definitely avoid the psychologically destructive representation of God in a Caucasian form (discussed in a later chapter). We must build and maintain strong, clean, and safe communities. The ability to influence our environments in some small way is the first step towards building or restoring self-respect.

Community Division

The point of this discussion is that slavery had and continues to have a devastating effect on the personalities of African-American people. There is much overlap and connection between these traits since they have all come out of the same situation. There is also wide variation as to the continued influence of these traits on different individuals, but certainly they persist to a lesser or greater extent within ourselves and within our communities.

One of the most serious disturbances of community advancement coming from the slavery experience is disunity or "community division." The age-old pattern of divide-and-conquer was utilized along with so many other tricks in order to destroy African-American community life. Wedges of division were thrown among the slaves in order to insure that the possibility for united efforts would be nearly impossible. The slave makers were fully aware that a disunited community would be easy prey for the continued control by the master. Therefore, all kinds of devices were utilized in order to make sure that the slaves would not be able to come together.

A speech delivered by a white slave trainer, William Lynch, on the bank of the James River in 1712 well illustrates this strategy:

> *...I have outlined a number of differences among the slaves; and I take these differences and make them bigger. I use fear, distrust and envy for control purposes. ...take this simple little list of differences, and think about them. On the top of my list is "age," but it is only there because it starts with "A." The second is "color" or shade. Then there is intelligence, size, sex, size of plantations, status on plantation, attitude of owners, whether the slaves live in the valley, on a hill, east, west, north, south, have fine or coarse hair or is tall or short. Now that you have a list of differences, I shall give you an outline of action. ...you must pitch the old Black against the young Black. ...you must use the dark skin slaves against the light skin slaves and the light skin slaves against the dark skin slaves. You must also have your white servants and overseers distrust all Blacks. But, it is necessary that your slaves trust and depend on us. They must love, respect and trust only us.*

Gentlemen, these kits are your keys to control. Use them. Have your wives and children use them. Never miss an opportunity. My plan is guaranteed, and the good thing is that if used intensely for one year, the slaves themselves will remain perpetually distrustful.[9]

There were major social divisions constructed by the master. The house workers and the field workers constituted the major separation among the slaves. Those slaves with the lesser physical load of the housework were taught by the master to see themselves as a privileged group. They were permitted to wear better clothes, eat slightly better foods and, most importantly, they were permitted to take care of the personal needs of the master and his household. Just to be physically close to the master gave the slave a sense of superiority over his fellow slaves. Stampp (1956) describes this phenomenon in the following way:

> *The slave holder needed the willing cooperation of some of his bondsmen to make his government work efficiently. Knowing that the majority could not be trusted, he tried to recruit a few who would be loyal to him and take his side against others. Usually, he found his allies among the domestics, skilled artisans, and foremen, all whom he encouraged to feel superior to and remain separate from the field hands...In this manner, some planters gained the assistance of chattels who identified themselves wholly with the master class.*[10]

The slaves who were the illegitimate offspring of the master were usually given greater privileges. Along with other house slaves, they were delegated authority over the field hands of the master. A tradition grew up giving those slaves with physical features like the slave masters a feeling of superiority over those slaves without such features. Stampp (1956) again observes:

> *But the most piteous device for seeking status in the slave community was that of boasting about the white ancestors or taking pride in a light complexion. In the eyes of the whites, the "mulatto" was tainted as much as the 'pure" Negro, and as hopelessly tied to the inferior caste; but this*

did not prevent some slaves of mixed ancestry (not all) from trying to make their Caucasian blood serve as a mark of superiority within their own caste.[11]

Among the house and field slaves, there was a constant designation and alternation of authority by the master in order to keep the community divided. Those given authority were made to believe that their welfare was dependent on the master's welfare, and that they were independent of their fellow slaves. Therefore, they worked against the development of any unity among the slaves.

The slaves with certain skills, such as iron workers, black-smiths or carpenters, were separated from the common field hands and made to believe that they were something quite special. All of these special categories of slaves were easily pitted against one another on the basis of their special classes or skills, which prevented them from dealing with their common status as a slave. Their total dependence on the slave holder essentially sealed their fate against their effective self-development. The inevitable conflict among them almost invariably worked for the benefit of the slave masters. The slaves' energies became consumed in affirming and defending their special class membership, rather than addressing their real problem: the condition of slavery. The master fostered such rivalries since such "false" issues effectively distracted from the "real" issue. It seems that William Lynch's kit worked like a charm and it is still effective almost 300 years later.

Divided communities among African-Americans persist. The sophistication of the classes dividing the community has improved and the classifications have multiplied tremendously. Rather than house versus field, it is fraternities, sororities, schools, churches, white-collar, blue-collar, republican, democrat, neighborhoods and hundreds of other bases for divisions. The root is simple, but the basis for the separation is the same: that is, to keep the community divided. The origin of all the classes, clubs, and groups sill come from the same source--an outsider who still profits from our division.

Though perhaps not intentional, the divisive outcome is the same. The deeply entrenched predisposition to accept division rather than unity within our communities is one of the most deadly outcomes of slavery. Every leader or scholar who has attempted to address African-American community problems poses this destructive dis-unity as the most deadly disease in our communities. On those fleeting occasions, when African-American communities have unified behind an issue, our potency as a people has been awesome. Perhaps it is the potential power of such unity which forces those who profit from the status quo, to feed the disunity among African-American people. One would hope that exposure of this "plantation ghost" to the light of knowledge would facilitate its rapid disappearance.

African-Americans now, as we did 300 years ago, still spend more time justifying our separate goals than we do working on our shared goals. We are usually incapable of addressing our common problems because we feel that our separate problems are more important. This is another one of those constantly repeating dramas from slavery which we continue to act out because we have not understood its origin in our not-so-distant slavery experience.

The Family

Probably the most serious effect of all was the impact that slavery had on the African-American family. The family is the very foundation of healthy, constructive, personal and community life. Without a strong family, individual life and community life are likely to become very unstable. The destruction or damage to the African-American was accomplished by destroying marriage, fatherhood and motherhood:

> *Slavery does away with fathers, as it does away with families. Slavery has no use for either fathers or families, and its laws do not recognize their existence in the social arrangement of the plantation. When they do exist, they are not the outgrowths of slavery, but are antagonistic to that system.*[12]

William Goodell (1853) describes the institution of marriage as it was viewed by the slave holders:

> *The slave has not rights, of course; he or she cannot have the rights of a husband, a wife. The slave is a chattel and chattels do not marry. The slave is not ranked among sentient beings, but among things, and things are not married.*[13]

Goodell continues in his graphic description of slave marriages:

> *The obligations of marriage are evidently inconsistent with the conditions of slavery, and cannot be performed by a slave. The husband promises to protect his wife and provide for her. The wife promises to be the helpmeet of her husband. They mutually promise to live with and cherish each other, until parted by death. But what can such promises by slaves mean? The legal relation of master and slave renders them void! It forbids the slave to protect even himself. It clothes his master with authority to bid him to inflict deadly blows on the woman he has sworn to protect. It prohibits his possession of any property wherewith to sustain her...It gives master unlimited control and full possession of her own person, and forbids her, on pains of death, to resist him, if he drags her to his bed! It severs the plighted pair at the will of their masters, occasionally or forever.[14]*

This description rather graphically illustrates the ultimate meaninglessness of marriage for the slaves. Even under circumstances where the marriage ties were not arbitrarily violated, the very condition of slavery contradicted much about the vital and fundamental conditions of marriage.

The African-American man was evaluated by his ability to endure strenuous work and to produce children. He was viewed by the slave master as a stud and a work horse. The stronger and more children he could sire, the greater the expansion of the master's slave holdings and the greater his financial worth. The more work the slave could perform, the greater the production, the greater were the profits that came to the master. African-American manhood was defined by his ability to impregnate a woman and the magnitude of his physical strength.

The virtues of being able to protect, support and provide for one's offspring, which is the cornerstone of true fatherhood, were not considered the mark of a man on the plantation. In fact, the slave who sought to assert such rights for his offspring was likely to be branded as a trouble-maker and either punished or killed. After several generations of such unnatural treatment, the African-American man adapted and began to resist the role of a true father.

Today in African-American communities around America, we carry the mark of the strong-armed stud from slavery. He occurs as the modern-day pimp or the man who delights in leaving neglected babies dispersed around town. He is the man who feels that he is a man only by his physical, violent or sexual exploits. He leaves welfare or chance to father his children--and he fathers his "ride," his "vines," or his "pad." This peculiar behavior is often characterized as a racial trait attributable to some type of moral weakness in African-American men. Such conclusions fail to identify the real origin of such characteristics. Such family irresponsibility does not occur among African people who have never endured the ravages of slavery or who were able to preserve their cultural integrity in spite of slavery.

The African-American woman was valued primarily as a breeder or sexual receptacle capable of having many healthy children. Again, Goodell (1853) offers an example of a newspaper advertisement for an African woman which demonstrates the desirable qualities of the slave woman:

> *A girl, about 20 years of age (raised in Virginia), and her two female children, one four and the other two years old, is remarkably strong and healthy, never having had a day's sickness, with the exception of the smallpox, in her life. The children are fine and healthy. She is very prolific in her generating qualities and affords a rare opportunity to any person who wishes to raise a family of healthy servants for their own use.*[15]

Her work as a human being was reduced to the particular financial value or personal pleasure she could hold for the master. As a breeder, she was to be mated with the plantation's strongest "studs" regardless of human attachment. She was also usually expected to be receptive to the sexual exploitation of the slave master, his relatives or friends. Goodell (1853) documents this point:

> *Forced concubinage of slave women with their masters and overseers, often coerced by the lash, contributed another class of facts, equally undesirable. Rape committed on a female slave is an offense not recognized by law!*[16]

Such abuse of African-American women began to damage the natural nurturing and dignity of motherhood. Children were conceived out of convenience for an oppressor--not even at the level of animal lust. The child was doomed to continue in the very conditions which had bred him/her. Many women either became abusive to their children or over-protective of them in response to such inhuman conditions.

Even today, we find too many frustrated young African-American women choosing to become breeders in their search for an identity. Too many of those young mothers become abusers of those children, or turn them into spoiled and irresponsible pimps by indulgently protecting them against a cruel world.

The massive confusion around sexual identity so often addressed in the African-American media and periodicals, has its foundation in the conditions of slavery. Men seeking to be men through physical exploits, sexual exploits or even violence, is predictable in a setting where natural avenues to manhood have been systematically blocked. Women will experience inevitable frustration of their natural feminine aspirations when the paths to natural womanhood have been blocked.

The historical images which we have inherited continue to sabotage many of our efforts for true manhood (fatherhood) and womanhood (motherhood). In nature and throughout the historical development of cultured people, the roles of man and father, woman and mother, have been inextricably bound. Only in instances of decaying culture, such as Ancient Greece, Rome, and modern Euro-America, has this bond been broken. With its break has come family dissolution, followed closely by total societal dissolution.

Although current attitudes and conditions (such as unemployment) feed these patterns and keep them growing, the origins of the African-American family problems rest in the plague of slavery. If we understand the historical origin of these roles and patterns, then perhaps we will refuse to play them any longer.

Color Discrimination

Certainly, there are few irrational influences from slavery that have persisted as well as this one. Although the prevalence of this color discrimination has had periods of decline, it keeps returning in a more insidious form each generation. Skin color became the code for social position. Of course those slaves who more closely resembled their slave masters in color, the more positive the traits assigned to them.

Of course the very condition of the African's slavery was determined on the basis of skin color. The failure of Caucasians and Native Americans to endure the physical abuse of involuntary servitude led to the more massive enslavement of the African. The contradiction that slavery presented for the supposedly "free and Christian nation" led to the justification of slavery as a divinely authorized activity. The African's black skin was considered as evidence for his cursed state to serve as a slave. Some misinterpreted Bible allegory regarding the "curse of Ham" was used to justify the inhuman treatment of the African who was wrongly assumed to be a descendant of Ham.

Therefore, dark skin color became equated with the reason for slavery. The skin color of the slave became associated with other kinds of subhuman traits. On the other hand, the slave master's pale skin became equated with supernatural human traits. In fact, God, all the Saints, and the entire heavenly hosts became identified with the pale skin. The logical conclusion of the abused, oppressed slave was that the basis for his condition was his skin color, and the way out of his condition was to change that color.

This deeply ingrained idea has persisted. Even today, there is an unnatural equation of Caucasian physical features with beauty, intelligence, authority, and so forth. Many African-Americans continue to assume that beauty, competence and worth are greater among their people with the most prominent Caucasian features. There are still vast sums of money spent yearly on skin lighteners, hair straighteners and wigs, in the frantic effort to change African-American physical features. "Good hair" and "nice features" are still thought to be those characteristics most like Caucasians. Contrary to popular belief, these attitudes have not changed substantially among African-American youth who have grown up since the "Black Power" movement of the 1960's.

Following the social movements of the sixties, another limb grew on the color-discrimination tree. There was an effort, on the part of some people, to equate African physical features with mental and moral superiority. The same confused mentality that had established black as inferior and white as superior, was evident in the effort to make black superior and white inferior. The perspective which limits the human makeup to its physical surface hue, is equally limited, regardless of perspective. One scholar has stated that "he who remains ignorant of history is doomed to repeat history." Certainly, the persistence of our psychological, social and economic dependence on the former slave holders is evidence of the validity of this adage. The intensity and brutality of the slave-making experience traumatized our social and human development. Though many writers have spoken of slavery, few scholars have addressed the continuity of the behaviors established in slavery as a continuing aspect of African-American psychology.

The one exception is probably Stanley Elkins (1968) who developed a sociological thesis that argued that the closed nature of North American slavery, in contrast to Latin American slavery, produced a "Sambo" type personality in the slave. The Sambo was described by Elkins as:

> *...docile but irresponsible, loyal but lazy, humble but chronically given to lying and stealing; his behavior was full of infantile silliness and his talk inflated with childish exaggeration. His relationship with his master was one of utter dependence and childlike attachment.*[17]

The problem with Elkins' analysis of the black personality, while identifying a possible outcome of slavery, is that he consumed his analysis into this single image. Our suggestion is of much greater complexity, but a similar recognition that the slavery situation produced some persisting personality traits.

The reader might inquire, with considerable basis, that if this discussion is correct, then the African-American personality has been devastated. One would expect the obvious taint of this humanly demoralizing experience to have affected all aspects and all members of this community. In fact, the vast majority of African-Americans operate with considerable efficiency and are generally no more severely disordered than are the people who were historically the perpetrators rather than the victims of these conditions. The fact that, despite slavery, such effective functioning is the rule, speaks to two factors which space will not permit adequate development in this discussion.

The first factor is the apparent strength of character, culture and heritage that African people apparently brought to America's plantations. Other people have degenerated in their fundamental humanity under conditions of stress far less intense and enduring than those experienced by African people. Research needs to identify the elements of that African character which might serve as a model for human strength in general.

The second factor is that survival of the fundamental human initiative among African-Americans, despite over 300 years of the most inhuman conditions ever experienced by any people in the current historical epoch, is indicative of human resilience at its best. Despite the lingering vestiges which we have described in this discussion, recovery has been substantial. The triumphs of America's former slaves far exceed the deficits attributed to us. African-American people exist more as a monument of human accomplishment than the remains of human destruction.

However, the fact remains, the "plantation ghost" still haunts us. Our progress is still impeded by many of the slavery-based characteristics which we have described previously. The objective of the discussion is not to cry "victim" and seek to excuse those self-destructive characteristics created by slavery. In fact, the objective is to identify the magnitude of the slavery trauma and to suggest the persistence of a post-slavery traumatic stress syndrome, which still affects the African-American personality. It is not a call to vindicate the cause of the condition, but to challenge Black people to recognize the symptoms of the condition and master it as we have mastered the original trauma.

Neither is this discussion an effort to underestimate the severity and barbarity of the continued economic and social exploitation of America's former slaves. It is to call our attention to an array of attitudes, habits and behaviors which clearly follow a direct lineage to slavery. It is hoped that by shining the lights of awareness on these dark recesses of our past, we can begin to conquer the ghosts which continue to haunt our personal and social lives. We can begin to move beyond the shackles of restricted human growth that have bound us since the kidnapping of "not so long ago."

In the next section, we shall look at the process of breaking the chains of slavery. We must understand that despite the impact of the slavery experience and the persistence of many of these characteristic slavery behaviors, African-Americans and other victims of this kind of oppression are not passive objects of their historical trauma.

Liberation from Mental Slavery

In order to address the problem of "breaking the chains of mental slavery," there is a simple but important idea that must be understood. This idea is actually true for all human beings but has special importance for the people in the current condition of Black people. This idea is that human beings are a very special form of creation; we have a very unique place in nature. We are the only life form in nature who operate based upon our *self-consciousness*. Every other form of animal life on this planet, no matter how gigantic or how small (whether it has the building precision of a termite or the destructive capacity of a rhinoceros) do what they do *not* based on what they know about themselves but guided by their instinct or innate programming. There is nothing which requires the worker bee to define itself as a worker bee in order for it to work in the hive. Insects, birds, and beasts do what they do based on instinct or training (adaptation). None of them acquire their abilities from any knowledge of who they are, at least so far as we have been able to observe .

This quality of creatures in nature has some drawbacks. On the one hand, these creatures are able to do what they do and not too much more other than what they are programmed to do. Ants have been building the same basic type of hills for thousands of years (with occasional modification to fit the changes which humanity has imposed on nature). They have not been able to progress beyond this form and they will probably be doing it the same way for thousands of years yet to come. Even though the form apparently serves them well, there is no evidence of any significant advancement in their hill-building skills over the centuries. We have no evidence that any other form of life on this planet has the capacity to make anything known as "progress" because they are locked into what they do very well but they can't do too much else.

As human beings, our limitations rest only in our ignorance. We are ignorant of who we are and what we can do. We have the need to gain consciousness (awareness) and only in consciousness is our true human capacity open to us. We are not a *tabula rasa* (or blank slate) at the time of birth but we must have the access code in order to gain the creativity of our God-given genius. The access code for other animal life forms is simply the stimulation of the environment and some minor training experiences. We must acquire consciousness of who we are and what we have been in order to operate to our full human capacity. This is why cultures expend so much energy in creating the kind of environments and experiences which insure that each generation of human beings will maintain the gains and acquire the consciousness which is necessary to preserve the human accomplishments. Human beings clearly have the deadly potential to drop below even the most despicable forms of barbarism and endanger the entirety of human advancement, even the most basic human characteristics. We are the only life form who can engage in collective and individual self-murder for no apparent transcendent motive while knowing the consequence of the suicidal act. Instinct prohibits such conduct among other forms of life. The rare occurrence of other animals committing suicide (such as whales beaching themselves) is undoubtedly a result of ecologically insensitive humans disrupting the natural environment which fouls up the natural instincts, rather than these behaviors being conscious self-murder. We can go lower than any form of life, but we also can go higher. This is the mixed blessing of freedom.

If this is the nature and mixed blessing of freedom, what must we identify as the source of human power? The answer is obvious. As we have suggested above, this ultimate human power is our mental power, our consciousness, our awareness. Whatever the form that consciousness may take will determine our state and circumstances as human beings.

By no means is this an original formulation. This perception is as old as there has been any remnant of human civilization. This has been known by *Homo Sapiens* (knowing beings) for as long as we have been *Homo Sapiens*. Human beings have consistently worked to create the circumstances to maximize their consciousness and to insure that each subsequent generation will know fully who and what they are. On the other hand, whenever human beings chose to oppress or capture other human beings, they also did all that they could do to undermine any expansion of consciousness by the oppressed. So, when a group who has power wants to maintain that power or wants to take over the power of others; when people want to make captives of other people, they operate with the very same assumptions. They understand that ultimately the control of the people was in the control of their thinking, in control of their minds, in control of their consciousness.

The process of enslavement was not simply the brute force of overcoming people who were militarily weaker and forcing them to operate under your influence. It was not simply the outcome of barbaric treatment of captives by assault, brutality, restricted movement and activity. The process of human slavery is ultimately a psychological process by which the mind of a people is gradually brought under the control of their captors and they become imprisoned by the loss of the consciousness (awareness) of themselves.

It is this process which completely altered the human conduct of African people for the last four centuries. The disruption of our consciousness-building processes and the imposition of an alien consciousness has reduced Africans from being major builders and contributors to world civilization to becoming totally dependent on other's civilization for any guide to human conduct. African-Americans are most notorious for their self-destructive conduct, which is indicative of the process of destroyed consciousness that we are describing here.

The case history of African-Americans is a dramatic illustration of how this process destroys the human power. Africans were the builders of pyramids, now we destroy our own homes in frustrated explosions of rage and irresponsibility. We reached high civilization through the dignified leadership of African queens and many of us have now become contemporary abusers of Black femininity. We introduced medicine and healing on the planet. Now we have become drug abusers and destroyers of our own lives. We have descended from scientists who studied the heavens to become clowns who degrade and brutalize ourselves for the entertainment of our captors. These processes could only occur as a result of the loss of our higher human awareness.

"Let us make slaves . . ."

How did the slave-makers accomplish this deadly feat? They engaged in a systematic process of dismantling any and all mechanisms that preserved the continuity of the African people. The African captives were separated from related language groups and were isolated from their most familiar selves. Any of the rituals which preserved the integrity of the African culture from marriages to funerals were forbidden and alien practices were substituted or none were permitted at all. They cut the tongues from the griots who tried in the quiet of night to remind the people that there was a continuity that reached beyond the fields which they had come to know in Jamaica, Bahia, Alabama, Georgia and Virginia. Griots tried to remind the people of difficult days which had already passed and how we had endured death from the environment and from the hands of our enemies of centuries past. They tried to keep the people reminded that there was hope even in the face of hopelessness. This story was stopped and the teller was called a trouble-maker and used as an example of the fate of those who dare to sustain the captive's story of salvation. Such storytellers were brutally killed or mutilated so that their story of African continuity could not be told.

Slave owners frequently snatched suckling infants from their mother's breast for fear that the natural empathy of the birth mother might communicate a message of resistance that would undermine their process of captivity. There was a kind of conspiracy to create a race of orphans, to intentionally breakdown the Black family. (It is so ironical that contemporary social scientists make such an issue of the breakdown of the Black family which did not begin to break down until some white families began to break it down for their objectives). As we discussed in the previous section, families were broken up at the whim of the slave master. In addition, Black men were forced to watch their wives, daughters, sisters and mothers raped by their owners. Such experiences effectively disrupted the sense of connection and recipro-cal protection that exists in the preservation of family systems. By undermining this loyalty and protective image for almost twenty generations or 400 years, one is able to create a painful alienation between men and women which continues to contaminate the recip-rocal respect that men and women must have for each other in order to develop and maintain families.

As we have discussed in earlier parts of this volume, the personal character of the former slaves was distorted in ways that even 130 years from legal emancipation we still carry the scars. The processes of brutality, humiliation, and deliberate ignorance continue to plague the personalities of America's former slaves in such a way that make us our major enemies here at the turn of the century. The psychological process of slave-making remains an inadequately under-stood and appreciated phenomena for its impact on the functioning of African-American persons and our communities. The challenge for those who would choose to be healers of Black life must be the removal of these psychological chains.

Strategies to Break the Chains of Slavery

It is important to understand as a primary rule that the restoration of African consciousness is a process that must be accom-plished primarily by African people. It is unrealistic to expect that the descendants of the slave masters will initiate and play the major role in the elimination of the mental shackles which were put in place by their ancestors. This is not a condemnation of European-American people. As was the case with the abolition of physical slavery, many white people played critical roles which facilitated the alleviation of the philosophical contradictions of legalized slavery in a "free" country. However, it was the impetus and the persistence of the former slaves themselves who took the radical posture to demand uncompromised elimination of the system of slavery. We are again reminded of the tension experienced between Frederick Douglass who was an escaped slave and his liberal white abolitionist friends who viewed many of his positions as being too extreme. Certainly, Nat Turner had no white allies in his forceful removal of the captor's boot from his neck.

So much of the European-American consciousness is based on its affirmation of greatness and superiority in contrast to the inferiority and wretchedness of Africans. This false security built into white supremacist culture clearly limits the role that European-Americans are capable of understanding or playing in the restoration of African consciousness. Whether whites play a role or not is not nearly as important as it is for Black people to understand that our ultimate mental liberation must be guided by our independent action and activity. We cannot operate with the expectation that our true liberation can only come when European-American people change *their* mentality. The elimination of white racism is *not* a necessary prerequisite for the liberation of the African mind. Black people cannot commit excessive energy to the effort to alter the attitudes and consciousness of white people with the assumption that this is the path to freedom. Certainly, the obstacles created by white supremacist institutions and attitudes cause great difficulties in the march to Black mental liberation. There is no doubt that if those obstacles were removed, progress would be much easier. It is evident after all of these centuries that it is unrealistic to expect this European-American white supremacist mentality is going to disappear anytime soon. White racism is a fact of life and we must strategize solutions which are independent of its initial elimination.

As we have discussed above, the primary objective to freeing the Black mind is to change the consciousness of Black people. This is not a simple nor a brief process. We must understand that the current consciousness of Black people is the consequence of over four centuries of direct intervention and even longer efforts to destroy the indigenous institutions of African people which developed and sustained their independent human consciousness. We cannot expect that this process will be reversed at the end of a year or by reading a book. Once we embark upon the journey, change has already begun and will continue so long as the direction is maintained. We dare not surrender and declare defeat if we don't immediately see the massive results that we would wish. We must understand that generations of unborn African people will be the true beneficiaries of this process.

Knowledge of Self

In order to change the African consciousness we must change the information that is in the African mind. We cannot equate awareness with information though information is the road map to awareness and it is a critical part of the process. The "knowledge of self" which was the foundation of the highly successful Black reform program of the Honorable Elijah Muhammad (1965) and the premise of Ancient African teachers in the Nile Valley over 4,000 years ago, still remains an essential ingredient of this process of mental liberation. A fundamental component of the chains which continue to handicap Black minds is the excessive and distorted information about white people and the absence of information about ourselves.

Consistent with the argument we have already made in this discussion, European-American people have done an admirable job of insuring that the content of their consciousness was well-informed about their greatness. The great stories of Louis XIV, Columbus, Napoleon, Queen Victoria, Copernicus, Galileo, the Greeks and the Romans are fundamental elements of the information system that we are given about European-American people. This barrage of information about European and American greatness is systematically given to themselves to insure that they maintain their consciousness of who they are. Quite accurately, they realize that unless their children are given information about themselves they will never develop the consciousness that will permit them to maintain their control and influence over the world's major resources and their actions of self-determination and survival within the human family. So the story about European accomplishments and the description of European culture and structuring the world's reality around European experiences are essential parts of building the European consciousness to insure its survival and maintain the freedom of European people.

We do not wish to argue in this discussion that European people are not in their rights to offer such information for the expansion and maintenance of their human consciousness in order to insure their self-interest. We do argue, however, that if this is the only information that African-Americans receive, then they develop an inordinate regard for the self-interest of European-Americans and inadequate or no regard for themselves or their own self-interest. Therefore, Black children need to know about Black accomplishments throughout history and throughout the world. They need to know about our heroes and heroines, our discoverers, scientists, teachers, artists, inventors and as much about the greatness of African accomplishment as Europeans are taught about the greatness of European accomplishment. Since our objective is not the captivity of Europeans nor the guiltless domination of them, this information about the African accomplishment should not exclude information about them (Europeans) and their accomplishments. We need to know about our great ideas, our great victories, but we need to also know about our great defeats and how those defeats were transitory and did not deter the forward progress of African people as a whole.

The great restoration project of especially the last 20 years has expanded and intensified the significant work that was begun by W. E. B. DuBois, J. A. Rogers, Carter G. Woodson, Martin Delaney, George G. M. James, and hundreds of others who realized the significance of reviving the history and telling the story of African accomplishment as a significant part of the Black liberation process. The continued work of the great scholars of the latter half of the 20th century such as Chancellor Williams, John G. Jackson, John Henrik Clarke, Yosef Ben Jochanon, Cheikh Anta Diop, Ivan Van Sertima, Asa Hilliard, Maulana Karenga, Wade Nobles, Frances Welsing, Molefi Asante, and many, many others will be remembered for generations to come as significant contributors to the rebuilding of the information about African and African-American reality that was erased by the distortions of slavery and the slave makers. Though there has been considerable controversy about the work of these scholars because they have dared to reveal what had been systematically concealed, they have made an invaluable contribution to breaking the chains whose strength had been fortified by the ignorance about our history and ourselves.

The demand for teaching about the Black experience is by no means a trivial consideration as has been claimed by white captors and Black captives alike. To change the content of the information is a necessary *start* to restoring the consciousness of Black people about themselves. It is not just a story of history, but a story of science and that every people have contributed to the progress of science and no one people has a monopoly on the accomplishments of science and technology. It is important that all people understand that the resources of the Earth are available to all of its inhabitants and the claims of superior knowledge, technology and circumstance is an accident of information and consciousness and not a Divine right given to some people and systematically kept away from others. The information about how Black people came to be in the state that we find ourselves is an important story to be told so that future generations will understand that it was not genetic deficiency and/or Divine decree which created our circumstances, but the advantage of human oppression that created the privilege of the few and the poverty of the many. This information begins to free our minds to let us know that there are no limits to our potential. When young Black boys learn that there are no limits to our possibilities on the basketball courts, we create the athletic genius of Michael Jordan or Magic Johnson and in their genius, they recreate the game of basketball. When our young people know that there are no limits to their potential in the world of manufacturing, communication, physics, chemistry or the science of the human mind, then those same young Black minds who create dances on the dance floor or compose music on their bodies with the "hand jive" will recreate these fields of human endeavor with the same incomparability.

Information about the Black reality and experience must be transmitted as broadly and as intensely as is possible. Black singers must sing about it, Black researchers must identify it, Black actors must act it, Black scholars must conceptualize it, Black teachers must teach it, and Black preachers must preach it. From the cradle to the grave, we must submerge ourselves in information about ourselves; from books, pictures and whatever source that will bring messages to our minds. Each bit of information helps to mold the keys which will open the chains that remain on our minds.

"Cel-e-bration Time, Come on!"

The popular musical group *Kool and the Gang* popularized this song in the early 80's. Even though they were singing about a rather transitory party experience, the lyric captures the imperative of a more generic process that is necessary to remove the chains of mental slavery.

We must learn to comfortably celebrate ourselves. Self-celebration (we again emphasize) does not necessitate the degradation of others. It does, unapologetically, sing the greatness of our accomplishments and special blessings to the world. It tells each new generation something about the value of the fabric from which they are made. Cultures and institutions put considerable resources into creating images and opportunities to sing the praises of their accomplishments. This process is an essential part of maintaining a free mind, but it becomes even more fundamental in freeing a captive mind. Certainly one of the major strategies for enslaving the mind was the degradation of the Black/African self. The story of natural Black inferiority and ugliness were constant stories told to destroy the worth of the Black mind. The fantasies of African backwardness as incapable of technological development and characterized by superstitious and humanly regressive acts of cannibalism and savagery were all constructed in Tarzan stories, Little Black Sambo images and thousands of other derogatory ideas and illustrations to destroy the Black person's self-image and to further the idea of Black incompetence and deficiency.

Celebration then becomes a healing. If Europeans could comfortably identify themselves with every image from Santa Claus to the Son of God in order to celebrate who they are, why shouldn't we find images (both real and imagined) that communicate to Black African people something about our potential greatness. Perhaps, Kwanzaa is not an actual African Holiday, but why shouldn't we have a week-long celebration that brings pride and dignity to our culture. Why shouldn't the entire nation stop on the second Monday in January to celebrate the battle for human dignity by Martin Luther King, Jr. If Black people decide to call an assembly of one million Black men in Washington, D.C., on a Monday in October 1995, then why question the celebration since the very structure of the city of D.C. so emphatically celebrates the greatness of European American accomplishment. The hundreds of statues, museums, galleries, libraries, plaques and monuments which blanket the city consistently celebrate the greatness of being European-American. One could very easily walk around D.C. for an entire day and conclude that only European-American males built this great country. It is not accidental that European-American males continue to run the country in that the celebration and information they receive continuously reinforces their greatness.

We must unashamedly display our images and great ancestral figures throughout our environments. From pictures on the walls to statues in the park and street names, we should celebrate our heritage and those people who have distinguished themselves as African people of greatness. We should have more than one street named for an African-American person, particularly in communities where we live; we should immortalize our great builders, thinkers, and warriors by constructing their images and placing their pictures systematically throughout our communities. Our churches should show pictures of great women and men of faith who endured to make a way for young Black people who had not yet been born. Although Biblical or Qur'anic heroes tell a distant story of the power of the faith, a greater story is told by our immediate ancestors who took the faith and changed not only the ancient world but our contemporary world as well. I would think that every Baptist church, at least, and every Black religious gathering place ideally should have pictures of Cynthia Westley, Addie Mae Collins, Denise McNair, Carol Robertson, these four Black girls who were killed when white terrorists threw a bomb through the window of 16th Street Baptist Church in Birmingham, Alabama, on September 15, 1963. They should be the angelic cherubims who we think of since their lives were lost in innocent worship in a church that stood for the dignity of their people.

As we discuss in greater detail in the next chapter of this volume if we must have images of religious characters, **let them look like us**. If we must have Santa Claus entering our houses on Christmas Eve and occupying our malls from early November until December 24, then make sure that your Black child has a fantasy of a Black Santa Claus who comes with goodies and good cheer from black hands and hearts. The mythology of the culture must celebrate ourselves as do the facts of the culture. The persuasion for this argument is demonstrated by looking around the world in any culture where people's minds are free and they engage in self-determined action, you will find that they comfortably celebrate themselves in hundreds of ways.

The family reunions which were initiated in such large numbers during the late 70's were an excellent and creative way to celebrate the Black family's worth, survival and expansion. The decoration of mantles and walls in Black homes with pictures of their children and their ancestors, though simple acts were profound efforts to carry on the celebration process as best we could in environments that we had some control over. We need to gain broader control of the environments that we occupy so we can expand those images of self-celebration. We should comfortably celebrate in our own churches, schools, or communities–the birthdays and history of significant ancestors who have paid a great cost for our freedom. This celebration should and must go on independent of permission being given by the outside political figures. Black History Month must be a *start* for the celebration of our being. It cannot be an exclusive celebration, but must continue from February 1 until January 31 the following year. This must be a right that we guard and make apologies to no one for maintaining.

It is through self-celebration that we heal our damaged self-esteem. Yes, feeling good about oneself is a legitimate activity of cultures. In fact, any culture which does not make its adherents feel good about themselves is a failure as a culture. It is through the energy of self-worth that humans are motivated to improve and perpetuate themselves. The inspiration for the greatest of human accomplishments in architecture, science, poetry, art, industry, or any other human endeavor has been fueled by the octane of self-worth and a positive self-esteem. In the same vein, the low point of human degradation and even human self-destruction, both personally and collectively, is a consequence of the absence of self-esteem which demoralizes the very human spirit. To free ourselves, we must comfortably celebrate ourselves!

Only the Brave Need Apply

The process of mental liberation is not unlike many of the requirements of physical liberation. Freedom from captivity must be *taken*, not passively requested. It is never willingly given since the captivity has been in some way beneficial to the captor, so the captor gives up his captive only reluctantly. As our great Ancestral Saints, Harriet Tubman, Nat Turner, Ida B. Wells, Frederick Douglass, Medgar Evers and many others (now nameless) all found out, the decision to take one's freedom meets with resistance and even mortal danger. To take the captor's trophy could easily result in death to the captive. The lonely and ill-equipped road to freedom is one that will be wrought with all kinds of dangers. It is one thing to sing songs of freedom and to dream dreams of one day having it, but to take the responsibility to claim one's freedom is not for the faint of heart.

The nature of the alien consciousness has already created an atmosphere which justifies your captivity both to themselves and to your fellow captives. You are viewed with suspicion of your sanity to even raise the issue of wanting to be anything other than a well-kept slave. Both your fellow captives and your master cannot possibly conceive why you are not content to partake of his benevolence on his plantation. When you have earned the status of a "privileged" slave (economically, educationally or favor from association with the master), then it becomes even more incredible that you should want any more from this life in this world. The first designation is that you are "crazy" to think of freeing your mind. You are encouraged to compare yourself with your captive ancestors who suffered such great distress and so many of your fellow captives who continue to suffer great agony and this should be sufficient evidence of your blessed status. The fact that you no longer have literal chains on your body is more than sufficient evidence that things are "changing" and you are only a greedy and impatient step short of heaven.

Once you are designated as "crazy" then your credibility is seriously compromised. No one who wants to be respected as sane would dare pay any attention to you. What's even worse is that "crazy" people are not be trusted to care for themselves and they must be carefully watched for fear they may be a danger to themselves or others. Since your insanity has been defined by someone with another consciousness with another set of objectives, then what constitutes a danger fits into their frame of reference and not into the reference of your free consciousness. Courage is needed to deal with the isolation and vulnerability which results from this designation by your captors. The fact that they control the consciousness of most of your fellow captives means you have very few allies who can offer support and even protection as you seek to free your mind.

The process of beginning to think new thoughts in a new consciousness is a lonely process. It has been described as going into the desert by the newly liberated "Children of Israel" in the Old Testament and the *Holy Qur'an*. It is described as going into the wilderness as did Jesus Christ after he was baptized (liberated) by John the Baptist. Each of these scriptural images speaks to the sense of isolation which comes from newfound freedom. The loneliness and vulnerability which comes from the removal of your chains and trying out your new legs is considerable. As was the wilderness experience for both the Hebrew Children and the Christ, there are strong temptations to relapse constantly confronting the newly freed mind in the desert. The reminder of the security and companionship that you knew as a captive is constantly thrown in front of you. The possibilities for fame and fortune if you will abort your new consciousness and come back into the captor's mind set is almost a daily consideration. So it is for those who would dare to free their minds from slavery. They see their less competent and infinitely less accomplished fellow captives rewarded extravagantly with fame, fortune and celebrity status simply by their confirmation that the master's consciousness and his reality is the correct way to think. One can receive grants, tenure, promotions, movie roles, television shows, book contracts, or just the fame of being a prominent display on master's centerpiece simply by disavowing the consciousness of freedom and comfortably staying on the confines of the mental plantation.

This is why those who would choose to break the chains of mental slavery must be courageous. Only the very brave can resist the temptations or endure the isolation. Since the new consciousness can take a lifetime to begin to show tangible results, it takes a great deal of courage to persist in breaking the chains of the old consciousness and developing a new consciousness. This is another area where the new information and the self-celebration becomes very important. You cannot rely upon the encouragement of the multitudes running to your support and defense. The very nature of the slave's mentality insures that the majority of the slaves will be primarily committed to their master and his consciousness. Though your very life is committed to freeing the minds of the captives, you will be perceived by them as an enemy and they will gladly surrender you to crucifixion for the nature of the enslaved mind demands it. This requires you to be patient and comfortable that what you know is correct and even with so much consensus that you are wrong, you must be able to hold on to your right of freedom. This takes great courage.

Rebellious slaves have always been dealt with in a very brutal fashion. In the days of the physical plantation, they were beaten, mutilated or killed. In later times, the same torture was the fate of those who threatened the status assigned to the former slaves. Even today, the possibility of imprisonment, police brutality, mysterious deaths from questionable causes is still the fate of those who challenge the master's consciousness. Of course, there are always the social murders of being unable to make a living, being publicly humiliated and accused of all kinds of horrendous crimes of reverse racism, anti-Semitism, un-American activity, etc., etc. The bottom line is that those who seek to get free are still dealt with severely and one should not take the decision to break the chains from your mind as a minor consideration. It will take courage.

How do we gain such courage? The more we know the braver we become. The stronger our pride and self-love, the greater our courage. We must maintain association with newly escaped slaves who know the price and the feeling of true mental liberation. There is strength in association. We must seek out colonies of maroons (or runaways) and gain solace from our association with like-minded souls. We must commune with the spirits of the ancestors who knew and took freedom before us and in anticipation of us. We must stand with the Paul Robeson, Marcus Garvey, Sojourner Truth, Fannie Lou Hamer, Elijah Muhammad, Harriet Tubman, and W. E. B. DuBois spirits who refused to settle for captivity in any form and whose entire lives were examples of the commitment to breaking the mental chains and going into the desert until they were free. The ultimate weapon against fear is faith, which we will discuss below.

Umoja or Unity

There is strength in solidarity with others who are seeking to break the chains. As we have discussed in earlier sections of this book, "community division" was one of the major weapons used against the slaves. The fact that so much effort has gone into making sure the slaves do not form a common identity is indicative of the value of such a common identity. As was demonstrated during the civil rights struggles of the 60's as well as the successful Million Man March of 1995, the most potent weapon that we have in developing any kind of independent freedom is through unity.

Breaking the mental chains of the slave requires us to stand together despite the definitions of division that we have been given under the slave's consciousness. We have discussed in the previous chapter, the impact of William Lynch's "kit" for the control of the slaves. As we gain greater knowledge and information, many of those divisions will disappear because they cannot stand under the light of Truth and correct information. We must see our membership in religious groups, political groups, professions, academic groups, even in gender and class groups as being devices which can be and continue to be used to keep us divided and at war with each other. Although there are certainly issues on which we differ based upon the experiences in these various groups and categories, we must realize all of those differences are secondary when it comes to the reality of breaking the chains. We can do this more effectively if we begin by allying ourselves with other Blacks in the various groups where we find ourselves. When we stand together with other Blacks in our religious or political groups, professions, or even gender groups, we find that we have much more in common as Black members of those groups than we do with our non-Black colleagues. This realization brings the point home very clearly that we must stand together on the basis of our racial realities. Once we are able to see the commonality of our issues in the groups where we have strong identities, then we will be able to form coalitions with Black people who are a part of groups that we may know nothing about or feel hostile towards. So different fraternity men stood together as Black men at the Million Man March; Black Republicans, Democrats and Socialists stood together; Black graduates from the Naval Academy and West Point stood together when they realized that the unifying reality of being Black men brought them together. In a similar vein, Maya Angelou, Rosa Parks, Betty Shabazz all stood together in solidarity with Ben Chavis, Jesse Jackson and Louis Farrakhan in recognition that even being called a "man's" march required them to unite regardless of gender.

This is the kind of unity which is critical to obtaining mental liberation. As we have noted above in our discussion of courage, it is not possible to get free alone. The chains are very heavy and are interconnected which requires us to free each other as we free ourselves. The frightening thing about unity for many of the slaves is the fact that they may lose special privileges they have been able to acquire by their uniqueness (e.g., they can sing, play some kind of ball, speak the language well, or they are one of those "only Blacks" in some kind of organization). We know that many of these kinds of concerns vanish once we make the commitment to break the chains in our minds. With that commitment, we are no longer interested in holding on to minor slave privileges. On the other hand, however, there are unique talents and qualities which we all have. In the process of liberation, it is important to recognize that *unity does not require uniformity*. We can stand together and preserve our separate qualities which serve to enhance further the objectives of freeing ourselves and all of our people. We cannot break the chains unless we appreciate our unique form of enslavement while not permitting that uniqueness to impede our unity with others who are trying to get free. At the same time, as we free ourselves, we must adapt our special gifts to enhance the liberation process.

In the process of uniting we bring our special gifts to the total process of breaking the chains. If you sing, then sing freedom songs; if you play ball, then play freedom ball; even if you tell jokes, laugh while breaking the chains as Dick Gregory and Bill Cosby have done. Never let your unique gift be used to keep yourself and the remainder of our people in slavery. In fact, this is one of the most popular strategies. There are so many musicians, comedians and scholars who are rewarded for bringing messages which continue to tighten the mental chains. The same special use that our captors make of our gifts, we can use to further our mental liberation. The key to the power of unity in this liberation process is that we must avoid the danger of letting ourselves be used to impede the freedom process. In these latter days of the 20th century, this is the major strategy of battle against our liberation. In a similar vein, we must appreciate the power of unity as the major instrument to break the chains which continue to inhibit our minds.

Evidence of Things Unseen

Probably the single most important quality used in the act of achieving physical liberation from slavery was the inner power to believe that freedom was possible. It took a strong compelling belief that even though you could not see freedom and how to reach it, you knew it was possible and you were willing to confront all odds to obtain it. This is the power of *faith* and it was the power of faith that took Harriet Tubman back and forth on her many trips on the underground railroad. It was faith that permitted the thousands who ran away and took their freedom and endured the dangers and the obstacles to reach their goal. It was faith that sustained those who did not run away to keep their spirit and dignity intact until (physical) freedom was achieved. It was faith that kept the brutalized slaves from not giving up. In much the same way, faith is necessary to achieve mental freedom as well.

The faith that we are describing does not apply to any particular religious expression, even though all religions are based on faith and are intended to cultivate faith. The faith must be a basic sense that *"everything will be all right,"* no matter how things might appear. Whether this certainty comes from belief in a Supreme Being or in a process like Karma, the person looking to obtain mental freedom must find something to give them a sense of faith—that everything will be all right. This sense may come directly from a belief in the new conscious-ness and the freedom it will bring and a conviction that no matter how hard the battle, the progress towards removing the chains is worth it. I am certain that many physical slaves made the flight to freedom just on the basis of faith that anything would be better than captivity and this faith was strong enough to sustain them in their struggle for liberation. Without a strong faith in something bigger than your master and yourself there is no way to engage in the struggle that is necessary to achieve freedom.

As we have stated above, it is faith that provides a shield from our fears. It is the belief that "everything will be all right" that feeds the courage we described as being so necessary in obtaining this mental freedom. It is through the power of faith that the mentally enslaved person can, in the image of Samson, break the chains which confine us. This is another of those instances where qualities we already have can be transformed to serve the purpose of our freedom. If our faith is already in a concept of God, who has dominion over all things, then like Harriet Tubman, Nat Turner and many others, we can use the faith we already have to sustain us in our efforts to get free. Now, if that faith is in the god of the chains or in the god of the person who put us in the chains then of course, that faith will do you no good in getting free. In fact, it was that kind of faith which made many slaves fear to take their freedom or even to believe that freedom was in violation of God. Such can also be the case in seeking mental freedom. Of course, it is particularly difficult when the slave believes his chains are decreed by God and God, then, has become the chains. In the next chapter, where we discuss the impact of religious images on our psychology, we will further analyze the potential dilemma created by faith in alien images.

Faith must be acquired from within. This is very much an individual task which must be accomplished by drawing upon the example and the inspiration of those who have faith. We can be taught about faith by those who know faith, but each of us must explore our inner self to discover the power of faith. We must be willing to search for the belief in a power higher than circumstance and to locate this "evidence of things unseen." One of the great discoveries which comes from gaining information about who we are as African people is the overwhelming and convincing evidence that faith has been the sustaining force which has brought us to where we are. Where other people may point to material or intellectual resources, our power has been in our spiritual resources and it is this realization that helps us to discover the power of faith and our potential for faith even if we have not yet discovered it.

The task of breaking the chains of mental slavery requires a great deal of faith. Faith gives us the patience to stick to the job of looking for our own reality. It gives us the determination to overcome the hold of the chains of the plantation mind which tend to increase their grip as we seek to free ourselves. Since the situation of slavery created such a void of information about the African reality and so effectively erased the African consciousness, then it requires a great deal of faith to pursue the restoration of this awareness. As we mentioned above, the ever-present opposition which says to the fleeing mental slave there is no reality other than the European-American consciousness, requires faith to keep us seeking and building. Certainly, it is faith that sustains us in the fear and loneliness of this lifelong search to help restore who we are.

"Let's Get to Work"

Each of us has to make the commitment to engage in the personal and collective job of freeing ourselves from mental slavery. The strategies we have outlined above which will assist us in changing our consciousness is a continuous process. We must work to re-educate ourselves and our young people by seeking and studying new *information* about ourselves. We must find every opportunity to celebrate ourselves and we must challenge the fear that causes us to hesitate in taking the chains out of our minds. We must work together and we must have faith that our struggle will be successful, regardless of the opposition.

The first step is acknowledgment of our slave mentality and the fact that we remain limited in our effectiveness because of the slavery experience. There are many African-Americans who will be unable to do this because the very nature of the mental slavery creates an illusion that we are free. Hopefully, this publication and many of the experiences that inevitably we will have, will help us reach this realization. We trust in the natural love that human beings have for freedom that will motivate us to break the chains once we realize they exist. As we have discussed above, we will immediately understand we cannot be freed just as individuals, but must work to free all of the mental captives. As we become aware of our captured mental state, then we will have to commit ourselves to join the mental liberation process for all Black people. The accomplishment of this task will become increasingly easy as we gain more and more people committed to this mental liberation struggle.

Racial Religious Imagery and Psychological Confusion

We have spent much of the last 100+ years since legal emancipation fighting what has been the surface of the problem. Because we were operating at the surface, we had no sooner cut down the upper limbs of racial oppression that the underbrush grew back, consuming us again. Our problems were literally "Sisyphian"--perpetually rolling the stone of social, political and psychologically resolution to the top, only to have it roll down, and we began the difficult cycle all over again.

You may read books such as *The Strange Career of Jim Crow* by C. Vann Woodward and discover that what is happening in the social and political environment right now, at the close of the 20th century, are essentially the same events which were occurring at the close of the 19th century. There was a similar time, about one hundred years ago, when African-American people thought that freedom had been acquired. With political enfranchisement and the aid of some other people helping us to set our agenda, we had more African-Americans in positions of political power one hundred years ago than we actually have today. Reconstruction in the South produced more political presence for African-Americans than we have had since.

The presence of African-Americans in positions of political power throughout the southern United States, and even in northern parts, was a common occurrence before the end of the 1800's. In less than ten years time, the Jim Crow laws were enacted and we found ourselves in almost the same political condition that we were in prior to 1865, or worse! After 1865, we had the illusion of freedom, which made the disenfranchisement even more cruel than to the slave who was clearly defined as "without rights." It took almost a hundred years to get the Jim Crow laws removed to bring us right back where we were one hundred years before. Then, along comes the political changes of the 1980's and 1990's, which have threatened to reverse many of the political gains made in the prior two decades. These changes are combined with a mentality that is not unlike the heavily racist one which had reached a fever pitch at the time of the establishment of the Jim Crow laws.

The fact that the clock can be so easily turned back, and we repeatedly find ourselves trying to correct problems which were supposedly resolved, may suggest that we are not appropriately recognizing and/or dealing with the real problem. Such relapses would not occur if we were not perhaps dealing with symptoms of the problem, or superficial manifestations of a deeper problem–which, like the weed whose root is left intact, soon rises again to choke the life from the garden of progress. The nature of our problem is quite serious and represents a deeply embedded psychological disturbance. We need something more than an aspirin to remove the symptoms. **We need massive corrective surgery on the brain!**

Religious Imagery

Modern students and scholars of the mind have not adequately dealt with the influence of religious symbols and imagery on the thinking of people. Certainly, ancient students of psychology, particularly those of the Nile Valley civilization in Ancient Africa, devoted considerable attention to the significance of symbols and images on the minds of people. In fact, the massive symbols which stand as monuments of this great civilization, such as the sphinx, the pyramids and obelisks were constructed with the specific intention of creating powerful and compelling images in the consciousness of people. Perhaps the European psychologist, Carl Jung, is a distinct exception to his European colleagues as he devoted considerable discussion and theoretical speculation regarding the importance of symbols in general and religious symbols, in particular, on the thinking of human beings. He argued for their relevance to psychological and mental well-being and also identified the impact of their absence or distortion. Jung did not (nor do any other European-American psychologist) discuss the specific impact of these racial religious images on the psyches of Black people.

It is important to keep in mind that the image of God, which a people or a person possesses will determine the potential limits of their minds. If people have a narrow image of God, then their minds are narrow. If people believe that the biggest reality is a tree, then that is the extent to which their minds can aspire. If one believes that God can be only as large as a river or a lake, then that is as large as that mind will be able to reach. Such an image prohibits you from conceiving of the ocean which feeds the lake, and if you cannot conceive of the clouds which feed the ocean, your potential for understanding "Truth" and the competence which comes from Truth is limited. People with a limited or narrowed concept of God, then, have an automatically limited and narrowed psychology.

If you have come from a small rural town and you have only played against 140-pound football players, and you won your varsity letter every year, then you really believe that you have great powers within that limited context. If you happen to find yourself at a major university where the lightest man on the team is 200 pounds, suddenly you are forced into another reality. Because your point of comparison was with 140-pounders, your capabilities are only understood within that limited context. If you were capable of doing more, you would not know it until you got into a broader sphere.

There is a young man I know who was a triple jumper on the university track team. For the entire year he had been trying to jump farther than his record he had set in that region, which was 52 feet. In each meet his competition would jump 47, 49 or 50 feet. He could not get beyond 52 feet because 52 was the best he could do under the pressures that were available, and his own record was the best image that he could find to influence him. He eventually went to the national meets, and the *fifth* place jumper jumped 53 feet! You can imagine what the first, second, third and fourth place jumpers had done. Suddenly, this young man, who had desperately reached for greater distance all year long, jumped 54 feet 6 inches–surpassing everything he had been able to jump all year, and he did it repeatedly throughout the entire meet.

What had happened for my friend was that his imagination had been expanded by his experience with *bigger images*; and his capacities had consequently been expanded. The implication of this is that the mind's possibilities are limited by its concept of its potential. Human potential is broadened or limited by its concept of God. Thus, if God is anything finite (that is, limited), then you have already limited your mind. However, if God is *infinite*--without limits, without boundaries, without deficits or definition, always "greater than"–you have already expanded your mind to reach for the limits of all things. Such a consciousness of God puts us into the proper field to grow to our greatest height.

This idea constitutes the basic reason why any finite image of God is in fact limiting to our psychology. The problem only multiplies as we begin to attribute other limited characteristics to the deity. But to have a concept of God that can be put into a limited frame, a limited image, or a limited idea, automatically limits what your mind can do and where your mind can go.

Imam Warith Deen Muhammad once stated in a public lecture that, "If you can put God into a frame, then you have got Him and He does not have you." He continued, "If you can hang Him up on your wall, He belongs to you; you do not belong to Him–you can take His picture, put it in a frame, lock Him up in a room, and do whatever you want to do." However, if God is going to be God the Ruler, the Creator, the Maker of all things, then He cannot be put into a limited frame.

The question of particular characteristics begins to raise a whole variety of questions. We could develop a discussion around any number of problems which arise from this anthropomorphic idea (that is, creating God in man's image). For example, there are considerable problems in making the deity "man" as opposed to "woman." If God is just a male, that means there are 50% of human possibilities that God is not. This means that you have cut off God's possibilities and limited your concept. You have introduced an unnatural psychology into those who are women who would see themselves less favored because God is of a different gender.

The purpose of this discussion is to look at a particular characteristic that has been assigned to God, and some of the consequences of that set of characteristics on the psychology of people everywhere that this image has gone. We want to study the impact of racial characteristics which have been attributed to God.

Impact on the Psychology of the Portrayed Race

There is a serious psychological problem created for the person portrayed in the form of the Divine image. Since the focus of our discussion will be the impact on those who are not so portrayed, it is important to begin with this perspective to suggest that the problem is clearly not uni-directional.

The person who looks up and sees his physical characteristics shared by the deity begins to develop the idea that he is exactly like God, or that God is limited to be like him. This is all right if one sees potential for growth within the idea. The confusion of the physical attributes with the very nature of God begins to make the person feel that his particular physical features have endowed him with automatic claims to divinity. Such a person can begin to believe, in his own mind, that "I am the God, I am the Deity, I am the Creator." He begins to believe that the blond hair and blue eyes on the portrait are his qualifications for divinity. This begins to cultivate an ego maniac. Such a person begins to suffer from ego inflation. This serves to create a monster incapable of correction or growth since they see themselves as already perfect.

Such thinking is very characteristic of paranoid persons--those people who believe that everybody or somebody is out to get them--which they explain as a consequence of their being superior to other people. They seriously misrepresent themselves, over-stating their own importance. This is a major characteristic of the mind which begins to believe it is actually the God.

Hitler, possessed by the image of a blue-eyed, blond-haired deity, was convinced that the Aryan race was the superior race and that everybody else needed to be destroyed. Napoleon could not rest until he had conquered and subdued the whole world, because he felt that he was like the Caucasian image that was exhibited throughout his society.

We can look at country after country--Belgium, Portugal, France, England (an empire where the sun never used to set)–and we find maniacal conquerors who felt they had a Divine right to rule because they were "like God." This is revealed in their conviction that conquering was necessary to civilize the "heathen, pagan, barbaric world," (meaning that "anybody who doesn't look like us is heathen because we are the ones who are the gods"). They were possessed by an unnatural and deluded image of themselves.

From the Amazon to the so-called "Middle East" we still find this assertion of Divine Right to own and rule. They think they are God! In Palestine, some refugees from Europe walked in and said, "God said this is our land, this is our Promised Land! Our God promised it to us, he looks like us and carries our national identity. This is our homeland and you are supposed to give in and submit." The ultimate story is that the image or concept of God being like a particular people endows them with an unnatural perspective on themselves and others.

Now, let us look at this very carefully. We do not want to suggest that God should not be conceived as One who can impact all people in any condition. We do not want to believe that somehow God is incapable of elevating all people. All men and women can be reached by God. We should not confuse God's ability to reach all of us with the belief that we are God.

The problem that has been created for the Euro-American mind, which has led him to become an imperialist, a slave master, a colonialist, an oppressor around the world, is rooted in this idea that made him believe he was the Caucasian image that he had identified as God. He believed this gave him the power and the right to do whatever he wanted. This destroyed their natural human humility and their submissiveness to the Superior God-Force. The idea of white supremacy suggests to Caucasian minds that they are the superior by nature.

One of the things that helps human beings modify their conduct, naturally, is an understanding that though they have great strength, they also have real limitations. One of the things that lets human beings come back into balance is a realization that there are things which naturally limit them. If you go too long, if you run too hard, you get tired and you have to come back and get some rest. If you eat too much, you get a stomach ache, and you know you should not eat so much. If you watch television too long, you get a headache and you know you should not watch so much of it. But, once people get an inflated idea of who they are and what they are, they do not have the capacity to naturally correct themselves. They begin to do things that ultimately destroy themselves.

One of the reasons that the use of intoxicants has led to so many disasters is because drunken drivers lose the natural capacity to correct themselves. Drunk drivers find themselves going 80 miles per hour, and they feel like they are only going 40 miles per hour. The drivers see a stop sign and think it is two blocks away. It's too late when they realize that they are upon it, they run the sign, hit and kill someone, and then the mistake is realized. The sober persons, with a realistic sense of who they are, are able to say, "Okay, here is the sign, let me stop." They see it, respond to it, act and do what is necessary. They are equipped to naturally correct themselves and regulate their behavior. But one of the things that happens when people unrealistically perceive what they are, they begin to create a situation whereby they cannot naturally correct themselves.

The European world is on the verge of self-destruction because it no longer has the capacity to correct itself. It has gotten somehow consumed by its own consumption because it cannot naturally correct and regulate itself. It has made itself hated by nations around the world because it cannot naturally correct its addiction to excess. They are drunk on the idea of being like the image that they portray as God.

The Effect of Racial Images on African-Americans

For African-Americans, racial religious imagery is even more devastating. We have demonstrated that the one who sees himself in the Divine image is given an unnatural and a very inflated notion of what he or she is, which develops a kind of egotistical maniac. What is even worse, though, is what happens to the one who is not portrayed in the Divine imagery and who worships a non-self in the image. In Judeo-Christian imagery, the Caucasian bows down and worships himself, and the African-American worships the Caucasian as a god as well.

Over a hundred years ago, a brilliant African Christian theologian and student of the social sciences wrote a very important document. It is a document that has been obscured by time because of the revolutionary and important insights contained in the document. Even African and African-American historians have failed to deal seriously with one of the most perceptive and brilliant historians in modern times. The Cambridge graduate, Edward Blyden, wrote the document entitled, *Islam, Christianity and The Negro in 1888.* He observed:

> *No one can deny the great aesthetic and moral advantages which have accrued to the Caucasian race from Christian art, through all of its stages of development, from the Good Shepherd of the Catacombs, to the Transfiguration of Raphael, from rough mosaics to the inexpressible delicacy and beauty of Gioto and Fra Angelico. But to the Negro, all these exquisite representations exhibited only the physical characteristics of a foreign race; and, while they tended to quicken the taste and refine the sensibilities of that (Caucasian) race, they had only a depressing influence upon the Negro who felt that he had neither part nor lot so far as his physical character was concerned in these splendid representations. A strict adherence to the letter of the Second Commandment would have been no drawback to the Negro. To him the painting and sculpture of Europe as instruments of education had been worse than failures. They have raised barriers in the way of his normal development. They have set before him models of imitation; and his very effort to conform to the canons of taste, thus practically suggested, has impaired, if not destroyed, his self-respect and has made him the weakling and creeper when he appears to Christian land.*
>
> *It was our lot not long ago to hear an illiterate Negro in a prayer meeting in New York entreat the deity to extend his "lily-white hands" and bless the waiting congregation.*

> *Another, with no greater amount of culture, preaching from John 3:2, "We shall be like Him," etc. He exclaimed, "Brethren, imagine a beautiful white man with blue eyes, rosy cheeks and flaxen hair, and we shall be like him." The conceptions of these worshippers were what they gathered from plastic and pictorial representations as well as from the characteristics of the dominant race around them.*[18]

It is important to note that Dr. Blyden, over a hundred years ago, was writing about the problem we are continuing to face today.

The most obvious problem which comes from the experience of seeing God in an image of somebody other than yourself is that it creates an idea that the image represented is superior and you are inferior. Once you have a concept that begins to make you believe you are not as good as other people, based upon the assumptions we have already established, your actions follow your mind. If you have your mind set in a certain way, your behavior follows precisely the program of your mind. The content of this program determines who we are and what we are. So, if you have internalized the view of the deity and the Creator as being in flesh, having a nationality and physical characteristics different from yourself, then you automatically assume that you are inferior in your own characteristics. The sense of inferiority is not in the form of "natural humility" which we discussed, but you begin to believe you have less human potential than one who looks like the image.

The stage is now set for the cycle of a self-fulfilling prophecy: You believe they are superior and you are inferior, and sure enough you will start acting inferior. You begin to dress inferior; you begin to feel inferior; you begin to think inferior; you begin to have families that are inferior; you become economically inferior; you become academically inferior. You begin to follow the program. The first psychological necessity of making someone into a slave is to make the person believe *he or she ought to be a slave.* One of the methods for making someone act in an inferior way is to convince him/her psychologically that he/she is inferior. Once that is done, the job is completed, because people proceed to live out the prophecy just as they should. This stands as the foundation of many other kinds of problems that such a people will face.

What's interesting is that Euro-American psychologists are fully aware of the impact that other images have on people's self-esteem. The psychological literature well documents this phenomenon. Research by both Euro-American psychologists and their students, and certain African-American psychologists, such as Dr. Kenneth Clark, support this notion.

As far back as 1939, Dr. Clark and his wife did a study and demonstrated that little Black children (as early as pre-school) faced a major psychological problem--they did not like being Black and did not see being Black in a very positive light.[19] The Clarks gave three-year-old children black dolls and white dolls and asked them, "Which of these dolls is pretty?" The children chose the blond-haired, blue-eyed Caucasian doll. When asked, "Which doll is smart?" The response was the same Caucasian doll. Asked, "Which one would you like to look like?" The same one! Asked, "Which one is ugly?" The one that looked like the three-year-old Black child was selected. This study was published in 1939. Ironically, this problem has been here for a very long time.

In the 1960's, a change came about. One of the first things that the Black activists began to question was the fact that the textbooks, the actors on the T.V. and in the movies, even the mannequins in the store windows, did not look like them. The Black sociologists, psychologists, theologians and educators said, "We must change these textbooks and make the books have characters that look like us." Hundreds of concerned Black scholars and activists produced all kinds of data to show that the school books needed not only little white Dick, Jane and Spot, but they needed little Black children as well. Everyone from department store merchants to Hollywood producers were warned that Blacks would not patronize them if our images were not represented in their products. Justifiably, we wanted Black faces wherever African-American people were being influenced.

The seriousness of the Caucasian religious imagery is revealed by the realization of the absence of concern about these images. Almost no one dealt with the representation of God and all of the heavenly host in Caucasian flesh.*

---

*The distinct exception is Rev. Albert Cleage, who established his Shrine of the Black Madonna Church in Detroit in the early 1960's, as a statement against the influence of this Caucasian image of God on African-Americans. Though he identified the authentic African contribution to Biblical history, he concluded by substituting a limiting Black image for the limited white image. We must admit that his innovation was more healthy psychologically than the prevalent white image.

They objected to Santa Claus; they objected to the Dick and Jane characters with no Black playmates; they objected to the fact that there were no lawyers, no doctors, no nurses, no professional people on the television. They objected to all these things, but they did not object to the fact that their children were sitting down at two years old (and younger) being taught, "This man with blond hair, blue eyes, pale skin, is the Savior of the world, who died for your sins and is your God."

Black children sit at their dinner tables where a Black daddy and a Black mamma have often overcome racist opposition to provide them with food, and over the table there hangs a picture to which they bow their heads, looking at twelve Caucasians sitting around their table at "The Last Supper." There sits "God's son" and all of his "closest companions" and not even the cook, the server, or the bus boy is shown to look like the Black family on whose wall this image hangs.

God's "mother" (the Madonna) is Caucasian and all of God's "friends" are portrayed as Caucasians. Michelangelo went all the way and portrayed God himself (in the ceiling of the Sistine Chapel) with a long white beard to match his long white face, and the heavenly hosts were all portrayed in the same flesh. Few people saw this as a problem! Instead, our activists attacked the problem of Dick and Jane books, mannequins or soap operas. There was a real hesitancy to address the problem's worst manifestation in the church.

Perhaps the most disturbing fact is that this Caucasian image of Divinity has become an unconsciously controlling factor in the psychology of African-Americans. Brilliant scholars of the mind, usually effectively critical, were unable to see this influence. Their fear of accepting it, even after it was pointed out, demonstrated the presence of a mental barrier against recognizing this issue. Some of the most verbal critics of racism and its consequences have been thoroughly incapable of addressing this issue. The evidence of the controlling influence of these images is in the inability of even the most radical thinkers to openly challenge what they had come to believe unconsciously was actually the image of God.

Now, if the experts had this problem, just imagine what your poor grandmother would have to endure. Imagine what your twelve-year-old son is dealing with, when he has already endured eleven years of Sunday school pictures. Imagine your personal dilemma when you must challenge your long-held image of the very face of God.

Let us understand that this problem has to be removed from the root. The image of God as a Caucasian is so pervasive in the society, that even one who may have never been in a church, would still be severely influenced by the image.

The assignment of particular characteristics to the Creator is one of the most destructive ideas in the world today. This is probably why even the sacred Judeo-Christian scriptures specifically enjoin, "Thou shalt not make unto thee any graven image, or any likeness of anything that is in heaven above, or that is in the earth beneath, that is in the water under the earth: thou shalt not bow down thyself to them, nor serve them."[20] And the *Qur'an* states, "Say, O People of the Book, come to common terms as between us and you: that we worship none but God; that we associate no partners with Him; that we erect not from among ourselves, lords and patrons other than God."[21]

Let us look at another quote from Edward Blyden in this regard:

> *Wherever the Negro is found in Christian land, his leading trait is not docility, instead it is servility. He is slow and unprogressive. Individuals here and there may be found of extraordinary intelligence, enterprise and energy, but there is no Christian community of Negroes anywhere which is self-reliant and independent. On the other hand, there are numerous Mohammedan (sic) communities and states in Africa which are self-reliant, productive, independent and dominant, supporting without the countenance or patronage of the parent country, Arabia, whence they derived their political, literary and ecclesiastical institutions.*[22]

So, it is said here, a hundred years ago by a Christian theologian, that the images of Christianity handicapped the productivity of non-white people accepting and worshipping white images of divinity.

Once you begin to believe that the deity is somebody other than you, then you are put into a psychological dependent state that renders you incapable of breaking loose until you break the hold of that image. Although we are 100 years out of slavery, we still govern none of the institutional forces that affect our lives. There is no successful independent Black (African-American) institution--that is, independent both in thought and economic control of the Euro-American ideas and institutions.

The frightening fact is that we control absolutely nothing! Our token presence on city councils, mayoral offices, or religious organizations does not mean that we are in control. We do not control the water flowing into the faucets. We do not control the lights. We do not control the buildings. We do not control the paved streets. We do not control the gas, the food–we do not control anything that affects our lives. Neither do we control the basic agenda or direction of any of these institutions.

Unfortunately, we often do not care that we don't control anything, and furthermore, we are defiant in preserving our dependence. If someone comes along and says, "Be independent." You say, "Oh, you are a radical, militant, revolutionary; get out of here." That person making such a suggestion is simply saying what a mama bird says to its baby birds ten days after they are born. And that is, "Stand (fly) on your own." If we say that to a people a hundred years up from slavery, and twenty thousand years into civilization, they respond, "I don't want to do anything like that." We begin to glorify dependence. We have become comfortable being governed by someone else. We are constantly looking for someone else to govern us.

Our dependent mentality and actual fear of autonomy leads us to even identify heroes on the basis of their dependence. A hero for us is one who begs more effectively than others. Our heroes are not admired for their independent thinking. We do not respect those people who are most effective in articulating our uniqueness and our capability for self-sufficiency. Instead, we revere people who prostrate themselves to other men on our behalf and gain the approval of our oppressors.

Distinguished African-American leaders, such as Marcus Garvey and Elijah Muhammad, are either ignored or condemned because they called for an independent view of ourselves as a people. Men such as these are treated as minor figures against great heroes who "begged" us into participation in European-American culture and institutions. Thomas Jefferson, Benjamin Franklin, Patrick Henry, and other Euro-American heroes were people who advocated American independence at all cost--even from their own mother country. Any African-American who makes a similar demand for African-American people is viewed with suspicion and/or hostility. The reason for this, at least in part, is because of the psychological dependence which has been fostered by acceptance of this image of God as Caucasian. Acceptance of this image makes it almost impossible to entertain an image of a self-managed cultural, economic or political life. People free of this influence do this quite naturally and quite successfully.

Of course, unchecked independence can lead to anarchy and imperialism. Those who identify with the image of God as self feel confident and correct in exploiting the resources of others. With such a mentality, one can comfortably take control over another's resources, because they feel that they have divinely given rights to do so. On the other hand, those under the influence of the alien image feel that they have no claim on any resources. The consequence is a persisting dependency which comes from the mentality that sees the Creator as being identified with another group.

One of the persisting difficulties facing African-American people is the difficulty to think independently. We are constrained by the perception that creativity and innovation are the exclusive privilege of those who are similar to the image of divinity. Our scholars are limited to imitating the scholarship of independent Caucasian thinkers. We analyze our situation and the nature of the world in general, exclusively from the frame of reference of Euro-Americans. We approach the solution of problems as if the nature of the problems of the former slave and descendants of African civilization are the same as those of former slave masters and immigrants from Europe. The consequence is a persistence of the more devastating problems that we have as a people, i.e., social, economic, political and motivational.

The image of the Creator sets the tone for the potential of creativity in the human sphere. Those who are alienated from the image of the Creator do not attribute strong characteristics of creativity to themselves. Therefore, productivity can at best be imitative of those who are viewed to be in the image of the Creator. Again, the problem stems from a stifled independence based upon the psychological straitjacket of seeing God portrayed as other then oneself.

Lacking in creativity, we are unable to go into our own experience and reap the benefits of our God-given gifts. We laud Freud, fail to see the value of our own psychological effectiveness in enduring the psychological traumas experienced collectively as an oppressed people. We adore Marx, but fail to recognize the superiority of our intuitive economic concepts which gave us economic sustenance through unity (i.e., synthesis), with minimal resources and in defiance of the Marxist dialectic. We proclaim Dewey's educational philosophy, while failing to articulate the dynamics of the feat of our own education in an environment which prohibited our very literacy. Our failure to study our own experiences and utilize the benefits of that experience, is a clear defect in our social effectiveness. Our lack of confidence in our unique experiences and reality has its root in our perception that we do not have equal access to the presence of the Creator because He does not look like us!.

Persistently haunted by this image of Divine, we consistently seek out leaders or authorities who resemble the appearance of the Caucasian image of Divinity. The real irony is the number of highly educated and intelligent African-Americans who are literally locked-in intellectually to the authority and intellectual leadership of non-African people. The authority may be Marx, Freud, Skinner, Gloria Steinheim or the Pope, but the underlying basis for the legitimacy of the "expert" is his or her similarity to the Caucasian religious images. This is not, however, to discredit the presence of viable and effective ideas in each of these and many other European and non-African thinkers. People are no more *denied* access to Truth by their color, than they are given "chosen" access to Truth by their color.

One problem for African-American advancement as a people is our tendency to reject the authority and leadership of those who do not have Caucasian features, and we rather faithfully and uncritically accept the leadership or authority of anyone who possesses those features. It is almost as if people with African features cannot be authorities unless they have been authenticated and credentialed by the highest European or Caucasian authorities. Only, then, is the non-Caucasian person viewed as an authority. The only exception to this rule is the situation of the fundamentalist minister whose claim to authority is that he "has been called." He then identifies the voice of his "calling" as being precisely this same Caucasian figure who can "wash you whiter than snow." This "called" representative is then given unbridled authority, even when he may not represent the self-interest of the people he is leading. This Divine representative can then have the legitimacy of the Caucasian "God," who is so highly revered. The point is the same, whether one is authorized by Harvard or a "call," the source of legitimization is identical.

Although the focus of this discussion has been on the situation of African-Americans, it is just as true in other cultures where the Euro-Caucasian image of Divinity has gone. The African nations most strongly under the influence of this alien image are least effective in determining their own destiny. They all have "experts" from the other nations telling them what to do, not only with their technology, but with their religion, their social and political philosophy as well. They have limited ability to exercise autonomy in self-government and in respect for indigenous leadership because the highest authority has been identified in non-African appearance.

Dr. Edward Blyden makes another relevant observation on the impact of elevating the Caucasian image of God:

> *The Christian Negro, abnormal in his development, pic-*
> *tures God and all beings remarkable for their moral and*
> *intellectual qualities with the physical characteristics of*
> *Europeans, and deems it an honor if he can approximate-*
> *-by a mixture of his blood, however irregularly achieved-*
> *-in outward appearance, at least, to the ideal thus forced*
> *upon him of the physical accompaniments of all excellence.*
> *In this way, he loses that "sense of the dignity of human*
> *nature" observable in his Mohammedan brother.*[23]

In other words, Dr. Blyden is suggesting that those Christians who have taken on the idea that the only way to be excellent is to be like a Caucasian, are the same people who believe the only qualities which are civilized qualities are those associated with Caucasians. Standards of excellence in family life, cultural life, moral life, dress, manners, language and everything are identified with them. "There is no dignity in being oneself," suggests Dr. Blyden.

Too often the conclusion is reached that the absence of some of these qualities among African-Americans and the persisting aping of European mannerisms and cultures represent a fundamental deficiency in the conduct of African people. The arguments suggesting an innate and genetically determined intellectual deficit among Black people are extensive and compelling. Many of these qualities of self-negation and inadequate social development of African people within a European context can be attributed directly as a consequence of the issues of this discussion. In this regard, Imam Warith Deen Muhammad raises a penetrating question:

> *What would happen to the minds of Caucasian people if*
> *Black people would suddenly come into power with their*
> *mentality and with their love for religion? What would*
> *happen if nappy-headed, Black Jesuses were put all over*
> *their land and throughout their homes, and in all of their*
> *churches? What would happen to their minds over a*
> *period of three hundred years if they kept coming to*

> *churches seeing our image as their redeemer, seeing our*
> *image as their prophets, their apostles, their angels? They*
> *would be reduced to inferiority because the image before*
> *them of the supreme model of superiority would be "black"*
> *and not "white."*[24]

Imam Muhammad places the problem in the broader context of a
psychological process in this hypothetical image. The influence of this
Caucasian image on the psyches of non-Caucasian people is no worse
than would be the influence of a Black image on the psyches of non-Black
people. The reduction of people to a state of inferiority represents a
reprehensible form of mind control of the worst kind. It also becomes
the basis of insuring the continued psychological enslavement of any
people under such an influence.

The Solution

There are two modes of attack on this psychologically crippling
influence faced by non-white people in Christian societies. One mode of
attack involves the removal of the images from the outer world and the
second involves the removal of the internalized images from the inner
being.

The removal of these images from the outer world was initiated
in the late 1970's by the thrust of Imam W. D. Muhammad and the
C.R.A.I.D. (Committee for the Removal of All Images that Portray
Divine) efforts of the (then) American Muslim Mission. By protests,
flyers, public rallies and publications, direct social action was taken to
raise this critical issue among religious people. There is probably no
more significant effort of social reform than this effort to "remove all
images and all racial effects from worship."[25]

Such political activity has real relevance in correcting the
environment's contribution to the problems which we have discussed
previously. Removing the images from the society can clearly protect
the young children from the influence of such images. We can protect
them from this influence on their thinking which makes them view
themselves in a distorted and unnatural way. The protection will serve
young Caucasian minds, who develop an unnaturally inflated image of
their self-worth, as well as the young non-Caucasian minds which see
themselves as inferior because of these images.

In the late 1980's Bishop George Augustus Stallings, at the time an African-American priest in Washington, D.C., began to challenge the Roman Catholic Church about its role in perpetuating white supremacist images. His active attempt to reflect African cultural experiences in liturgy, images, and symbols of the Catholic church led to his eventual resignation from the Roman Catholic Church and his founding of the African-American Catholic Congregation, which affirmed the African-American culture and addressed the relevant needs of the African-American Catholic Communicants. He subsequently established a national appeal for all Christians to declare a "Black Church, Black Christ." This became an effort that he initiated to encourage all Black Christian congregations to discontinue the portrayal of Christ or other Biblical characters in Caucasian flesh. For several years he has held national conventions and campaigns to eliminate Caucasian images from Black churches and Black worship.

Our scholars who address the social and psychological functioning of African-American people must take up this issue as one for their scholarship and research. African-Jamaican cultural scientist and psychologist, Leachim Semaj[26] and others have done some preliminary investigations which demonstrate that young children have a conception that "God is white" (University of West Indies, 1980). Such research is critical in beginning to uncover the destructive psychological influences which distort our thinking and our living.

Professional organizations dedicated to the unique problems of African-Americans must take forthright positions on this issue as well. As the *American Medical Society* is the voice of authority on health in the Western world, the professional groups of African-Americans must be the voice of authority on the mental, social, economic and political health of African-Americans. Such an effort has already been initiated by the *National Association of Black Psychologists* in a resolution which the world's largest organization of non-Caucasian mental health experts adopted in 1980 (See appendix). This resolution condemned the presence of Caucasian images of Divinity as psychologically destructive to the minds of African-Americans. Although the resolution passed with some difficulty, the slim majority which accepted it took a landmark stand against the most psychologically dehumanizing and inferiorizing influence in the society. There is a critical need for our experts to monitor more carefully the destructive influences in our physical, mental, social and spiritual environments.

The real challenge, however, is to remove the racial images of Divinity from our own minds. The long-term subjugation to this image on a subliminal basis has deeply entrenched its influence in our perceptions. The subconscious internalization will make it difficult to recognize its influence. Developing an awareness that the influence of these images is there, is the first accomplishment and the social, organizational and scholarly efforts described previously will facilitate this process.

But we must also take self-affirmative steps to transform our own world. We must carefully monitor the images to which we expose ourselves that perpetuate this destructive influence. For example, we might choose to refrain from uncritically watching a movie such as "The Bible," which depicts the entire religious history of the Judeo-Christian world in Caucasian flesh. We must begin to build institutions which preserve the reality of our own experiences. We must begin to develop educational materials, artistic productions, economic structures, fashions and concepts which deny the implication of our inferiority.

Our religious leaders must help us to learn that God (Allah, Jah, Jehovah, Yahweh, etc.) deals with all of us directly! There is but one Creator who has chosen all of creation within which to manifest His/Her greatness. We have the same responsibility as any other people to develop our independent powers while interacting cooperatively with others. Dependence on others' resources, ideas, and creativity is not necessary when people come to recognize the same potential that the Creator has given to each of us. We need not beg anyone if we realize the value of gifts we have been given and begin to utilize them as others do in a self-affirmative fashion.

This realization and these efforts will equip us to begin to overcome the last remaining stronghold on our psychological enslavement. Genuine emancipation of African-American people will not be possible until every vestige of Caucasian association with Divinity has been removed. Ultimate liberation does not involve substituting an African (Black) racial image for the Caucasian one. Ultimate liberation recognizes that the form of the Creator is a form superior to human flesh (totally) and the perfected being invites us to a transformed state of perfection larger than material identity. Such transformation will never be possible so long as our aspiration is locked in the frame of a material and (by implication) deficient or incomplete form.

Appendix

Endnotes

[1]Clark, C. "Black Studies or the Study of Black People in R. Jones," *Black Psychology* (1st ed.). New York: Harper & Row, 1972.

[2]Stampp, K. *The Peculiar Institution: Slavery in the Ante-Bellum South*. New York: Vintage Books, 1956, p.79.

[3]Douglass, F. *My Bondage and My Freedom*. Chicago: Johnson Publishing Company, 1855/1970, p.81.

[4]Stampp, pp.35-36.

[5]Douglass, p.78.

[6]Stampp, p.289.

[7]Douglass, p.76.

[8]Woodson, Carter G. "The Miseducation of the Negro," *The Crisis*. August 1931, p.266.

[9]Lynch, W. "The Slave Consultants Narrative." Source unknown, 1712.

[10]Stampp, p.151.

[11]Stampp, p.339.

[12]Douglass, p.39.

[13]Goodell, W. *The African Slave Code*. New York: American and Foreign Anti-Slavery Society, 1835, p.105.

[14]Goodell, p.107.

[15]Goodell, p.84.

[16]Goodell, p.86.

[17]Elkins, S. M. *Slavery* (2nd ed.). Chicago: University of Chicago Press, 1968, p.83.

[18]Blyden, E. *Christianity, Islam and the Negro Race*. London: W. B. Whittingham, 1888, pp.17-18.

[19]Clark, K. & M. P. Clark. "The Development of Consciousness of Self, and the Emergence of Racial Identification in Negro Pre-School Children." *Journal of Social Psychology*, 1939, 10:591.

[20]Exodus 20:4-5, *Holy Bible*, King James Version.

[21]*Holy Qur'an*, 3:64, Yusuf Ali Translation.

[22]Blyden, p.12.

[23]Blyden, p.18.

[24]Muhammad, W. D. "A Message of Concern to the American People." Chicago: *American Muslim Journal*, regular feature, 1980-1983.

[25]Ibid.

[26]Semaj, L. *Race and Identity and Children of the African Diaspora: Contributions of Rastafari*, unpublished manuscript. The University of the West Indies (Kingston), 1980.

Bibliography

Blyden, E. *Christianity, Islam and the Negro Race*. London: W. B. Whittingham, 1888.

Clark, C. "Black Studies or the Study of Black People in R. Jones," *Black Psychology* (1st ed.). New York: Harper & Row, 1972.

Clark, K. & M. P. Clark. "The Development of Consciousness of Self, and the Emergence of Racial Identification in Negro Pre-School Children." *Journal of Social Psychology*, 1939.

Douglass, F. *My Bondage and My Freedom*. Chicago: Johnson Publishing Company, 1855/1970.

Elkins, S. M. *Slavery* (2nd ed.). Chicago: University of Chicago Press, 1968.

Goodell, W. *The African Slave Code*. New York: American and Foreign Anti-Slavery Society, 1835.

Holy Bible, King James Version

Holy Qur'an, Yusuf Ali Translation.

Lynch, W. "The Slave Consultants Narrative." Source unknown, 1712.

Muhammad, E. *Message to the Black Man in America*. Chicago: Muhammad Mosque of Islam #2, 1965.

Muhammad, W. D. "A Message of Concern to the American People." Chicago: *American Muslim Journal*, regular feature, 1980-1983.

Semaj, L. *Race and Identity and Children of the African Diaspora: Contributions of Rastafari*, unpublished manuscript. The University of the West Indies (Kingston), 1980.

Stampp, K. *The Peculiar Institution: Slavery in the Ante-Bellum South*. New York: Vintage Books, 1956.

Woodson, Carter G. "The Miseducation of the Negro," *The Crisis*. August 1931.

RESOLUTION

APPROVED AT THE 1980 ANNUAL MEETING OF THE ASSOCIA-TION OF BLACK PSYCHOLOGISTS

WHEREAS: The display of the Divine in images of Caucasian flesh constitutes an oppressive instrument destructive to the self-esteem of Black people throughout the world and is directly destructive to the psychological well-being of Black children;

WHEREAS: The Association of Black Psychologists has condemned the negative portrayal of Blacks in media presentations in the past, we recognize the portrayal of the Divine as Caucasian as the most pervasive assertion of white supremacy. We see such grandiosity on the part of Caucasian people as destructive to themselves and damaging to people who accept white supremacy images as subliminal elements of their religious beliefs;

WHEREAS: There is a negative psychological impact when images of the Divinity and Divine figures are portrayed in Caucasian flesh with Caucasoid features, The Association of Black Psychologists considers such portrayal as being a mechanism which insidiously advocates white supremacy and by implication Black inferiority.

WHEREAS: The Association of Black Psychologists, as practicing experts in human mental functioning, recognizes that the persistent exposure to such images is particularly damaging to Black minds, both young and old.

THEREFORE, BE IT RESOLVED: That The Association of Black Psychologists recommends the removal of Caucasoid images of the Divinity from public display and from places of worship, particularly in settings where young Black minds are likely to be exposed.

RESOLVED: That The Association of Black Psychologists provide copies of this resolution to national religious bodies, national civil rights organizations, and to select religious leaders for the purpose of opening up an educational dialogue for change.

Other publications by *Dr. Na'im Akbar*:

The Community of Self
From Miseducation to Education
Light from Ancient Africa
Natural Psychology and Human Transformation
Visions for Black Men

Audio and video cassettes of *Dr. Akbar's* lectures are
also available from:

Mind Productions & Associates, Inc.
P. O. Box 11221
Tallahassee, FL 32302
1-800-662-MIND

Web Page Address: *www.mindpro.com*
E-Mail Address: *mindpro@mindpro.com*

———————◆———————